REPUTATION MANAGEMENT

WHAT A BUSINESS OWNER

REALLY NEEDS TO KNOW

By

Ian Turner

Thanks to the thousands of business owners and entrepreneurs I've met over the years that have shared their fears, passions, problems and successes with me.

And, good look to millions of entrepreneurs and business owners that are willing to risk it all in pursuit of a dream.

About the Author

Ian Turner is both a serial entrepreneur, business coach, author and speaker. Having spent the best part of thirty years involved in solving the problems of small to mid-sized businesses, he's got the insight of a well-honed expert business strategist.

Ian's one-on-one heartfelt approach doesn't mean it's softly softly. It's anything but! It means he understands the pressure people face when they make the decision to go into business for themselves.

What makes Ian Turner different? The business owner's challenges are considered personal challenges. When you've worked with thousands of business owners over the years that are facing catastrophic challenges it has to be personal, according to Ian. Ian Turner's goal is to help small business owners build better, stronger businesses that make a positive impact on everyone involved. Families, employees and communities.

Staying true to his sense of community Ian also helps non-profits.

i

Respected by business owners, attorneys and accountants alike for his ability to steer a client through crisis of every kind. Ian still coaches and writes for small business.

Other book titles by Ian Turner

How to Make Your Small Business a Big Success

Millions of people worldwide are either thinking about going into business for themselves or they are already in business for themselves. For many different reasons people choose a goal of independence, freedom and possibly the financial rewards of success without first thinking through the many *what-if's* that can lead to business failure.

If we start thinking about *the business of the business* we have the power to create the business we want. Most entrepreneurs, and small business owners start thinking and working in the business before they ever figured out the business of the business.

Most small businesses struggle to survive every day and they don't have to. This book is going to help us create an unforgettable roadmap to success.

How to Save a Small Business

When a business is in trouble, the last thing you need is a book full of technical jargon to read, understand, hypothesis, and philosophize over. When you're feeling the most pressure of your life because your family has been seriously hurt in an accident it's not the time to go study for a medical exam. It's time to take action.

The only way to save a business is by realizing a sense of urgency around changes that have to be made. The number one hindrance to saving a business is the business owner themselves. They leave it too late or they want to make minimal changes and then wait to see how it goes. The "How to Save a Small Business" book isn't about extending the pain of killing a business slowly. It's all about handling the emergency and getting you back to health.

You can find more information about Ian Turner at:

www.howtogetsmallbusinesshelp.com

www.facebook.com/author/ianturner

www.facebook.com/pages/How-To-Get-Small-Business-Helpcom

www.amazon.com/author/ianturner

Table of Contents

Preface

I don't know if there is anything that brings a small business to its knees faster than a reputation management problem! And the scariest thing of all, is that whatever is being said, written or communicated about a business or person doesn't need to be true. Not one word needs to be true to force the eventual closure of a business.

Do the laws change from country to country? Yes. Does it make a difference? Not really. If a business owner is going to use the law as their defense against online criticism – real or not – they are going to have a long fight ahead. It could take years and still the business is no better defended. The sad reality is that there are plenty of attorneys, SEO providers, advisors of every kind, and reputation management companies that will tell the damaged parties that there is plenty that they, *the professional* can do to solve the problem, quickly, efficiently, cleanly and for any given amount of money that fits the budget, Until it doesn't and the damaged party either cuts off the money or the damaged party loses the business because of unsustainable losses.

That doesn't mean there's nothing we can do. There's a lot we can do to both prevent a reputation problem and also a number of things we can do once we have a problem.

Don't be sold into the easy fix. There's nothing easy about managing your way through a reputation problem. On the flip side, when we start how we finish it sure does get easier.

This book will prepare you to defend, protect and change your reputation.

REPUTATION MANAGEMENT

WHAT A BUSINESS OWNER
REALLY NEEDS TO KNOW

Chapter 1. Let's begin by understanding the real problem

82% of consumers have stopped doing business with a company as a result of a negative experience.

79% of consumers that had a negative experience with a company told others about it.

49% of consumers said they would be willing to go back to a company after a negative experience if they were offered proof of enhanced service.

Actually, we should take a step even further back and recognize that there are two main reasons for wanting to know more about reputation management:

You want to avoid reputation damage

You are already reputation damaged

Everything that follows will still apply to both groups. If your reputation is clean – fantastic! Let's understand the world in which reputation management comes into play and do everything we can to keep the reputation we want.

If your reputation is already tarnished, especially by a high-profile destroyer, you want to get straight to the solution.

Here's the hard truth: if your reputation is already targeted by a reputation destroyer there is no getting straight to a solution. There is no magic potion. No miracle SEO, reputation management, or legal cure.

If your reputation is already targeted you just became prey to a host of potion-sellers. Stay with me till the end and you'll learn how to navigate the road you're on.

It's easy to blame a handful of negative posts on the Internet as the catalyst of a business failure. Left unchecked, reputation mismanagement can be catastrophic for a business. In the emotional moment where a company is faced with criticism (rightly or wrongly), business owners are becoming focused on completely the wrong problem. The main focus becomes the removal of the negative posting which can be almost impossible. There are plenty of companies that will promise to achieve whatever the business owner wants as long as the business owner is paying for the effort. It's not going to stop the next posting, nor is it going to minimize the damage already done.

Spending all of your time, effort and money on trying to remove negative posts (comments) is like digging for fool's gold! Some of the complaint sites and forums are both powerful and huge. They carry a number of characteristics that will help them rank high on a search engine. And, to top it all, the negative post normally has an intriguing headline that human nature can't resist clicking on to learn more!

You can't build or save a reputation by just trying to "cover up" or "push down" the negative posts. Try holding onto a cork under water. What is the cork trying to do with all its natural energy? Fight, to the top!

What happens when you let go of the cork? It goes right back to the top, no matter how much water you put on top of it. That cork is your negative post. Every time you relax your hold for a moment, that post is coming back to the top. Trying to just push down or bury a negative post is a defensive strategy. You can't survive by just being defensive. Where is the preventive strategy?

In order to succeed in business today we have to first understand what's changed. It's time to get old fashioned in a new world.

With the onset of the Internet, consumers, employees, and anyone else with access to the Internet are free to search, find, purchase, post, research, review, offer opinions and do anything else they choose to do – all from the comfort of wherever they choose to log on, and under whatever name they choose to use.

It wasn't that long ago that a business served a more specific localized area and knew its consumers. If a consumer wanted to say something positive or negative, it was possibly expressed to the business and verbally to a handful of local individuals. If the consumer didn't like the experience they received with a business they were faced with a decision: go somewhere else or – based on convenience – suck it up and begrudge the fact that it is still more convenient to purchase from the business they are unhappy with.

Previously, when justified or not, if a consumer had a complaint only a few people would hear about it and it was momentary. It wasn't written down for public display and commentary. It wasn't lasting, so if you had the majority of your consumers saying good things and returning to you for your products and services, they would drown out any comments made by an isolated unhappy consumer.

Think about what's changed.

Consumers can now purchase the majority of products and services from an expanded geographical region. Even when consumers are local they still go to the Internet to compare, review, price and judge a business against its competition. What are they using as a comparison? Anything that's available on the Internet. Real or not, if it's written it is giving a consumer a reason to use or not use a business' products and services.

In the absence of good news it takes very little bad news to cause a consumer to look elsewhere for a solution to their needs.

Bad news sells.

It changes perceptions, it doesn't need to be validated to be effective, and it gathers its own momentum and volume. Good news takes work, it takes effort, and it takes a deliberate plan and philosophy to overcome the bad news.

From an employee's perspective it used to be that employees became loyal to a business because loyalty was deserved. Most employees felt secure in their futures, knowing if they did what was expected or required they would have a place to be compensated for their efforts. Disgruntled employees would share their concerns with management and with other employees and friends. As said earlier, the concerns were not written down or placed for public display.

Most businesses had mostly good employees who were happy; every business had an employee that wasn't as good as they needed to be, and subsequently every business had or has an unhappy employee.

Over the last few years as technology changed the face of business, an emphasis on economics over philosophy and psychology took place, technology removed or minimized human interactions, customer service became a department and then the department was cut!

Employees became numbers that were easily replaceable, management motivations were unclear, and expenses were cut, cut and cut some more. Declining revenues became the norm and were historically and wrongly, for most, acknowledged to be the result of a declining economy. Businesses lost profit margins as they would cut the price of products and services as a means to compete. Eventually businesses cut themselves out of existence. Employees were faced with disappointment and loyalty became a forced expectation rather than something earned.

You cannot build a first-class consumer experience when you have a third-class employee experience.

What used to be localized verbal feedback in the moment is now public feedback. Feedback is almost permanent in nature and viral. It spreads publicly and often relatively minor issues become major ones. In the absence of strategy, the Internet has given power to the anonymous minority to influence the perception of the majority.

There is no question that Fortune 500 companies have already started to look at business differently and it's working for them. They are taking old-fashioned, traditional practices and applying new tools and tricks.

Here's an example of what they already know:

A Customer Experience Impact Report conducted by Harris Interactive points out the following highlights:

- The fifth annual report cited that 82% of consumers have stopped doing business with a company as a result of a negative experience

- 55% became a customer of a company because of their reputation for great customer service

- 40% began purchasing from a competitive brand simply because of their reputation for great customer service

- 85% of consumers said they would be willing to pay more over the standard price in order to ensure a superior

7

customer experience, of which 55% would pay 10% or more

- 55% of consumers recommend a company because of its customer service, compared to products at 49% and price at 42%

- 79% of consumers that had a negative experience with a company told others about it;

    1. 85% wanted to warn others about the pitfalls of doing business with that company

    2. 66% wanted to discourage others from buying from that company

    3. 55% wanted to vent anger or disappointment

- 92% of consumers said they would be willing to go back to a company after a negative experience if they;

    1. Received a follow-up apology/correction (63%)

2. Were offered a discount (52%)

3. Or were offered proof of enhanced customer service (49%)

- Online feedback influenced 49% of consumers' buying decisions

Of those who stopped doing business with a company:

73% was a reaction to rude staff

51% reacted to unknowledgeable staff

55% were because of issues that weren't resolved in a timely manner

Running a company the right way increases your top- and bottom-line. It makes a company more competitive. It makes a company more stable and more profitable.

Simply concentrating on defensive strategies means giving up control to external influences over which a business has no control. It's a recipe for disaster. Companies that do not have a preemptive strategy will find it difficult to survive in such a socially networked world.

The Internet opened up a world of opportunity for businesses and individuals alike. It also opened up a world of problems when strategies haven't been adopted to keep up with the changing face of business. Traditional brick-and-mortar stores do not need to become e-commerce companies to prosper in today's or tomorrow's market. However, they do need to adapt to today's market and the adaptation is simple when understood. Every company has the power to influence their external perception by controlling the inside of their business.

Does it offer a guarantee against the extremely malicious intent of those out to hurt you? No! Your online defense depends largely on where you are in the world. While some countries' legal systems take a more active role in protecting the rights of the defamed, the United States leaves the defamed with really no ability to protect themselves or a method to seek appropriate recourse against the anonymous poster and the host site.

Chapter 2. Free Speech isn't an excuse for bad behavior

First let me say that free speech is worth fighting for. No one wants to give up free speech. Any discussion relating to free speech turns quickly into an emotional one. Any attempt to change or reduce it in some minor way is looked at as the beginning of the end of free speech and a reduction in human rights.

In my simple world, hate groups such as the Ku Klux Klan wouldn't be able to voice their opinions or hide behind a mask while showing a public display of hate. Plenty of what I, or even the majority of people, consider radically unacceptable speech or opinion would be shut down or at least censored. But that's in my simple world based on an emotional response. The trouble is that when I add logic to the scenario, life becomes more complicated.

At what point do I or others stop censoring others' opinions? Who decides what should be shut down or censored? What if it's our opinion that is threatened? Freedom of speech hasn't always existed and the dynamics are always changing.

Free speech should come with responsibility, but it doesn't. Free speech is as much an ideal as it is a right. I don't want to censor someone's right to speak freely. Let them have their say, even if I disagree with their opinion.

But forgetting the legal arguments that could be made for what I'm about to hypothesize, let's think about the human rights of the victim for a moment.

Does the KKK have the right to come and terrorize me, burn a cross or stand in my front yard with a mask on? What if the law said that while as long as he/she wears the mask you can't prosecute them; they are immune or protected.

Does the guy that breaks into my house to murder my family have more rights if he wears a mask? What if the law said that while as long as he/she wears the mask you can't prosecute them; they are immune or protected?

Does the guy that wants to rob the bank say, "Just give me your money; as you can see I'm wearing a nice mask which is designed to keep me anonymous"? By anonymous does that mean the law said while as long as he/she wears the mask you can't prosecute them; they are immune or protected?

It appears that in an online world, this is exactly how it works. As long as you remain anonymous, which is aided by the host site, the anonymous party and the host become technically immune – untouchable by law.

What if I get drunk one night and argue with my neighbor, so I sneak out in the middle of the night and attach a poster to a board, naming my neighbor to be guilty of child molestation, and then place the board on the side of the street in front of my neighbor's house; what would happen to me? No one saw me do it and I wasn't stupid enough to put my name on it (at least not where everyone can see it).

What if the ground the board is on is protected and no one has to remove the board by law? What if lots of other people start placing their boards and posters on the same protected spot of ground? What if the person that owns that ground is now being paid a lot of money by advertisers to place their adverts around the boards because a lot of people are drawn to the sensational nature of the boards? What if other people that have never met my neighbor now think he's guilty and say he messed with their kids too (even if they have no kids)? What should my neighbor be able to do?

Sue me? He can't prove it was me! Even though every bone in his body says it was me. He can't prove it's me. The ground I put that board on doesn't have to give him access to the board, and furthermore the people that own the ground are encouraged to destroy any trace of my identity.

What if I sober up and in a moment of guilty reflection for the damage I've done to my neighbor, I sneak back onto the ground and remove my board? Sorry, it's not my board anymore and no one is going to let me take it down.

My point to all of this is that it isn't really about free speech. I am all for free speech. I am also all for having the right to know who my accuser is. Before the online world was afforded Sec 230 of the Communications Decency Act, it was a U.S. Constitutional right and in light of false or damaging propaganda in a criminal case we had the right to seek legal restraint from both the accuser and the place or publisher to which he propagated the information.

There is a catch-22 to the Sixth Amendment to the U.S. Constitution that states "In all criminal prosecutions, the accused shall enjoy the right to a speedy and public trial, by an impartial jury of the State and district wherein the crime shall have been committed, which district shall have been previously ascertained by law, and to be informed of the nature and cause of the accusation; to be confronted with the witnesses against him; to have compulsory process for obtaining witnesses in his favor, and to have the Assistance of Counsel for his defense."

The catch-22 is that this all relates to "criminal prosecutions." You may find it difficult, if not impossible, to start a case against an anonymous party. No one technically took away the right to face your accuser or to seek criminal or civil remedies. Sec 230 just put a huge obstacle in your way of learning who the accuser is. Sec 230 also removed liability from the host for what the anonymous party said on the host site. Tell me that's not a perfect storm set for abuse.

In order to have Yin you have to have Yang. Without those willing to fight for free speech we all lose it. In order to seek balance to anything there has to be opposites. I may not agree with half of what they say and I'm sure they wouldn't agree with everything I say.

With every side to an argument when it becomes large enough there will be those who quietly fight for their opinion, and those who radically defend their opinion.

While I don't agree with some of the opinions or methods of persuasion used by groups such as the Electronic Frontier Foundation (EFF, www.eff.org), they are a necessary voice. The EFF is a political force, supported by over sixty thousand concerned citizens. That's quite a voice.

I know after being on the receiving end of some painful, misguided actions by groups claiming to be protecting the freedom of speech, there are some real whacky and vengeful propagandists who will do or say anything to win their argument. When both sides treat the other as enemies, guess what you're seen as? Enemies vehemently opposed to each other's views. In reality though we are not vehemently opposed on most views.

Learn how to listen first and talk second. Freedom of speech and organizations like the Electronic Frontier Foundation are all relevant to our way of life and enjoyment of life.

Chapter 3. About the Electronic Frontier Foundation (EFF)

Taking a very wide paintbrush to paint the EFF in a completely negative manner isn't the smartest thing a person could do. Privacy issues are incredibly complex. Electronic issues around privacy are becoming increasingly challenging.

You have governments and corporations deciding what is private and what's not – officially and unofficially. Think about the recent issues facing Facebook, wiretapping, monitoring your online activity, data gathering, GPS tracking...

The EFF doesn't just fight to protect bloggers' rights; it fights to protect the rights of us all.

In their own words taken from the EFF:

From the Internet to the smartphone, technologies are transforming our society and empowering us as speakers, citizens, creators, and consumers. When our freedoms in the networked world come under attack, the Electronic Frontier Foundation (EFF) is the first line of defense. EFF broke new ground when it was founded in 1990 – well before the Internet was on most people's radar – and continues to confront cutting-edge issues defending free speech, privacy, innovation, and consumer rights today. From the beginning, EFF has championed the public interest in every critical battle affecting digital rights.

Blending the expertise of lawyers, policy analysts, activists, and technologists, EFF achieves significant victories on behalf of consumers and the general public. EFF fights for freedom primarily in the courts, bringing and defending lawsuits even when that means taking on the U.S. government or large corporations. By mobilizing more than 61,000 concerned citizens through our Action Center, EFF beats back bad legislation. In addition to advising policymakers, EFF educates the press and public.

EFF is a donor-funded nonprofit and depends on your support to continue successfully defending your digital rights.

If you're a blogger, this page is for you.

One of EFF's goals is to give you a basic roadmap to the legal issues you may confront as a blogger, to let you know you have rights, and to encourage you to blog freely with the knowledge that your legitimate speech is protected.

To that end, we have created the Legal Guide for Bloggers, a collection of blogger-specific FAQs addressing everything from fair use to defamation law to workplace whistle-blowing.

In addition, EFF continues to battle for bloggers' rights in the courtroom:

Bloggers can be journalists (and journalists can be bloggers).

We're battling for legal and institutional recognition that if you engage in journalism, you're a journalist, with all of the attendant rights, privileges, and protections (See *Apple v. Does.*)

Bloggers are entitled to free speech.

We're working to shield you from frivolous or abusive threats and lawsuits. Internet bullies shouldn't use copyright, libel, or other claims to chill your legitimate speech (See *OPG v. Diebold.*)

Bloggers have the right to political speech.

We're working with a number of other public-interest organizations to ensure that the Federal Election Commission (FEC) doesn't gag bloggers' election-related speech. We argue that the FEC should adopt a presumption against the regulation of election-related speech by individuals on the Internet, and interpret the existing media exemption to apply to online media outlets that provide news reporting and commentary regarding an election – including blogs (See our joint comments to the FEC.)

Bloggers have the right to stay anonymous.

We're continuing our battle to protect and preserve your constitutional right to anonymous speech online, including providing a guide to help you with strategies for keeping your identity private when you blog (See How to Blog Safely (About Work or Anything Else).)

Bloggers have freedom from liability for hosting speech the same way other web hosts do.

We're working to strengthen Sec 230 liability protections under the Communications Decency Act (CDA) while spreading the word that bloggers are entitled to them (See *Barrett v. Rosenthal*.)

Section 230 protections

The Bloggers' FAQ on Section 230 Protections discusses a powerful federal law that gives you, as a web host, protection against legal claims arising from hosting information written by third parties.

What is this "Section 230" thing anyway?

Section 230 refers to Section 230 of Title 47 of the United States Code (47 USC § 230). It was passed as part of the much-maligned Communications Decency Act of 1996. Many aspects of the CDA were unconstitutional restrictions of freedom of speech (and, with EFF's help, struck down by the Supreme Court), but this section survived and has been a valuable defense for Internet intermediaries ever since.

What protection does Section 230 provide?

Section 230 says that "No provider or user of an interactive computer service shall be treated as the publisher or speaker of any information provided by another information content provider." This federal law preempts any state laws to the contrary: "[n]o cause of action may be brought and no liability may be imposed under any State or local law that is inconsistent with this section." The courts have repeatedly rejected attempts to limit the reach of Section 230 to "traditional" Internet service providers, instead treating many diverse entities as "interactive computer service providers."

How does Section 230 apply to bloggers?

Bloggers can be both a provider and a user of interactive computer services. Bloggers are users when they create and edit blogs through a service provider, and they are providers to the extent that they allow third parties to add comments or other material to their blogs.

Your readers' comments, entries written by guest bloggers, tips sent by email, and information provided to you through an RSS feed would all likely be considered information provided by another content provider. This would mean that you would not be held liable for defamatory statements contained in it. However, if you selected the third-party information yourself, no court has ruled whether this information would be considered "provided" to you. One court has limited Section 230 immunity to situations in which the originator "furnished it to the provider or user under circumstances in which a reasonable person...would conclude that the information was provided for publication on the Internet...."

So if you are actively going out and gathering data on your own, then republishing it on your blog, we cannot guarantee that Section 230 would shield you from liability. But we believe that Section 230 should cover information a blogger has selected from other blogs or elsewhere on the Internet, since the originator provided the information for publication to the world. However, no court has ruled on this.

Do I lose Section 230 immunity if I edit the content?

Courts have held that Section 230 prevents you from being held liable even if you exercise the usual prerogative of publishers to edit the material you publish. You may also delete entire posts. However, you may still be held responsible for information you provide in commentary or through editing. For example, if you edit the statement, "Fred is not a criminal" to remove the word "not," a court might find that you have sufficiently contributed to the content to take it as your own. Likewise, if you link to an article, but provide a defamatory comment with the link, you may not qualify for the immunity.

The courts have not clarified the line between acceptable editing and the point at which you become the "information content provider." To the extent that your edits or comment change the meaning of the information, and the new meaning is defamatory, you may lose the protection of Section 230.

Is Section 230 limited to defamation?

No. It has been used to protect intermediaries against claims of negligent misrepresentation, interference with business expectancy, breach of contract, intentional nuisance, violations of federal civil rights, and emotional distress. It protected against a state cause of action for violating a statute that forbids dealers in autographed sports items from misrepresenting those items as authentically autographed. It extends to unfair competition laws. It protected a library from being held liable for misuse of public funds, nuisance, and premises liability for providing computers allowing access to pornography.

Wow, is there anything Section 230 can't do?

Yes. It does not apply to federal criminal law, intellectual property law, and electronic communications privacy law.

What are some key Section 230 cases?

EFF has an archive of some of the key cases addressing Section 230.

Do blog or online forum operators have a legal obligation to post acceptable use guidelines for commenters?

No. Courts have held that Section 230 allows, but does not require, hosts to establish (and implement) standards of acceptable use without risking liability for doing so. But posting guidelines is still a good idea, since people will often appreciate some guidance of what is or is not acceptable.

Are blog or online forum operators legally obliged to hold to their policies?

Probably not. Most acceptable use policies give the host wide latitude over what editorial actions they take and are not presented in the form of a binding contract.

Can my commenters sue me for editing or deleting their comments on my blog?

Generally no, if you are not the government. Section 230 protects a blog host from liability for "any action voluntarily taken in good faith to restrict access to or availability of material that the provider or user considers to be obscene, lewd, lascivious, filthy, excessively violent, harassing, or otherwise objectionable, whether or not such material is constitutionally protected." This would include editing or deleting posts you consider objectionable, even if those posts would be protected by the First Amendment against *government* censorship.

Sweet, I can edit the comments on my blog to change the meaning and make commenters I don't like seem like crazed defamers.

Not so fast. As noted above, Section 230 protects actions taken in good faith, and you may be liable for new information you create. The ability to edit comments is strongly protected, but you should not abuse that power.

Chapter 4. Reputation management is never clear-cut when it comes to the law

In a nutshell, H.R. 1981, "Protecting Children from Internet Pornographers Act" of 2011 sure was creating a lot of fuss.

The bill was passed by the House Judiciary Committee and appeared to be taking away some of the opportunities afforded by the Communications Decency Act of 1996. In short there is a provision stating that the "provider of an electronic communication service or remote computing service shall retain for a period of at least 12 months the temporarily assigned network addresses the service assigns to each account."

In short then, an ISP would have maintained our records of activity for 12 months. Furthermore the information would be available for administrative subpoena – the records can be made available for discovery and civil prosecution.

Ok, some of you are jumping for joy crying, "Finally!" Others are crying about an infringement on our rights.

First of all, if someone is logged on to an open public Wi-Fi network, the IP address is traced back to simply a public box and not to the individual user. Secondly, doesn't this bill only apply to electronic communication services operating within American jurisdiction?

The last time I looked we were living with the World Wide Web, not the U.S.-only wide web. Would anyone prefer, say, North Korean policy? I didn't think so!

Just how long would it take before sites that fear the implications of H.R. 1981 are up and running outside of the jurisdictional boundaries?

It's against federal law in the U.S. for websites to take sports bets over the Internet. It's also illegal for banks to handle online gambling transactions. Do you see any shortage of online gambling sites? So, how long will it take before sites that fear the implications of H.R. 1981 are up and running outside of the jurisdictional boundaries? Does zero downtime sound about right?

Free speech is worth protecting and that means the speech I disagree with too. It might be shameful to say, but it doesn't matter who's right and who's wrong when fighting reputation issues.

Reputation management is not going to be solved just by changing the law. The world has changed and business needs to catch up with some old-fashioned values and some great new tools. For what it's worth, H.R. 1981 never made it into law.

Chapter 5. Is Google being paid to look the other way?

First, be careful what you wish for! When thrown into the reputation nightmares that can come from the Internet, one of the initial responses is to ask Google to take the offending link down.

Once you finally track down a way of contacting Google, you do it nicely at first as evidenced by your naivety, believing Google will and should listen to your request. You soon come to find out your request isn't going to be easily followed. You can't talk to someone by phone; you must email a generic address with your concerns.

You send the email and wait for a response from Google, and you wait and you wait. You typically won't get a response. There are a number of detractors of Google because of their general lack of what appears to be compassion for your plight. Google knows they are big enough to ignore you and they are also big enough to deal with your anger and still stay in business. Your anger is wasted on Google.

Google has, I would imagine, hundreds of attorneys and they can create a solid wall of legal defense that you cannot climb over. The Communications Decency Act (CDA), also referred to as Title V of the Telecommunications Act of 1996, Sec 230, gives Google and others that legal wall. Google spends millions of dollars on legal fees every year and while it isn't all spent defending their right to present search results as they deem fit, enough of it is for them to know how to defend what they're doing.

I've got to be honest, I hated Google for what I considered to be the perpetuator and profiteer of unethical business practices. If Google knew something was damaging and false why wouldn't they take a site down – unless they just didn't care who got screwed? I have read many an online article about Google's relationships with those who profit from running the anonymous posting sites such as www.RipoffReport.com. One such article by 97th floor titled "Google, Your Honeymoon with Ripoff Report has to stop" made some interesting points about Google's Terms of Service and Ripoff's use of certain SEO tactics.

I stayed focused on Google the wrong way for way too long, which made me powerless to see the real problem. I tried being nice with Google and got no response. I heard from our attorney who was buddies with some Google attorneys that, "First of all they really are nice guys" – I didn't believe him. And secondly, that "if a court asked Google to either take down or block access to a site even temporarily on our behalf, then they would be happy to oblige." Fair enough. I still wasn't focused on the right stuff. I was still angry at Google.

We went down the legal road and that's another story that didn't end well for us, so Google never took down or blocked access to any site or content. We hit Sec 230 and the world changed. For years I had continued to think poorly about Google and this guy, *Matt Cutts* who seemed to crop up as being involved in a number of these conversations. Who the heck is Matt Cutts anyway? Well, I used to think he was Google's Chief of Police. Or at least I did when I was battling things from the wrong end.

He's the guy we want to have on our side, taking down what we say to be fake, false, damaging content about us. His staff is/was a fraction of the size or resources of the legal department. Matt Cutts, I apologize for not thinking well of you in the past.

I had a eureka moment after reading a thesis by Madeleine Rodriguez. It was about 130 pages of her honors thesis while at Boston College. It wasn't the first time I'd been open to various interpretations and philosophical arguments about Google's role in the world; but it was the first time I started to think clearly about what I and others were really asking Google to do when I asked them to "be nice, trust me, I'm telling the truth, the other guys are telling lies."

It's pretty stupid when you think about it. And maybe you did and you realized it a lot sooner than I did.

Google isn't who you want policing content. Matt Cutts isn't the Chief of Google's Police. Google doesn't have police, at least not in this regard. Matt Cutts who I have followed (socially online, nice guy) isn't who you want policing content, or Ripoff Report and every other copycat or negative trash site that has been in existence or will be in existence. Think about what we might be asking for: Google, we would please like you to take everyone at their word and act at their request. I know it might get a bit confusing if both sides lobby requests against each other; *oh, now who should you side with? Just trust me.* Here's another great idea: Google and everyone else, let's bring back a gentlemen's agreement – a handshake in place of contracts because everyone is honest and well-intentioned!

It's easy to get mixed up in intellectual and philosophical discussions about Google's role in this problem; we can continue to fall into the trap of paying someone to bang our heads into the same wall over and over, expecting to get a different result. Google, Bing and whoever comes next is the last entity you want policing what goes up on a search engine. How long would it take before you then accuse Google of restricting your freedom of speech? That's another story.

The court has the responsibility to ask things of Google and others of what must or should be complied with on behalf of the citizens it represents. If we don't like the scope the courts have to work with because of the law, we have to change the law. That's another story.

If we stopped looking to blame someone else for the problem, it may allow us to start thinking clearly about a solution. Small- to middle-sized businesses don't have the same resources as large companies or the amount of content and constant chatter about them that large companies do. All of which aid the large companies' ability to recover more quickly from a reputation onslaught. That doesn't mean the average business owner doesn't stand a chance against a reputation onslaught, they absolutely do. They just have to start thinking more clearly.

Chapter 6. The Google engine

Hopefully you will have moved away from wanting to throw something at Google for doing what we really want them to do, which is provide relevant information when we search for something through their search engine. *Remember we have choices of search engines.*

It's their search engine. We use it if we choose to. What we have to do is understand the reasons Google do what they do.

What's in it for Google? Google returns information for free. We think of Google like a public service, but, it's not! It's a for-profit company.

The last time I checked Google is a publicly traded company which means you have the right to buy as much of Google as you can afford and vote your shares as you wish. As a publicly traded company Google has a fiduciary responsibility to its shareholders. That means in basic terms that Google needs to drive up its share price. As a publicly traded company it means their financial statements are also publicly available.

How does Google make money? Primarily from advertising. I've seen statements on the Internet saying as much as 97% of Google's revenue comes from advertising. Think about

34

this: Google has created nothing but a giant marketplace and I don't mean that lightly.

Google is the library or bookstore of choice today. Want something in the reference section, it's over here. Want something on the history of Zen, it's over here. Want something on any subject you can think of and it's over here. All nicely organized, at least most of the time. Does someone sneak in and change the cover of a book once in a while or write obscenities over the pages? Yes.

It's a library. The library is open to the public! Crazy people or just different people go to the library just like we do. They even put books in the library that some of us find offensive and when they do some people say close the library as it could be harmful. Some say censor the library, put limitations on what they can and cannot put on the shelves. Don't give access to that book... Does this sound familiar?

Google built a more efficient library and we've been going ever since. What's in it for them? Well, they figured out if they put the time and money into building and maintaining a better library, they should be able to sell advertising space on its walls. Then they started to sell advertising within the books themselves. Google also brokers advertising space for you and me. 97% of everything Google does is for advertising dollars. No matter how they tie the bow on the box, it's still advertising dollars.

I don't care that Google makes money from advertising. What I do care about is whether they offer a fair and equal opportunity of search results ranking for those who contribute to their advertising revenue as to those who don't. I know Google openly frowns on keyword stuffing but on one page of a notorious "consumer advocacy" site that happens to have major Google ad space, an image containing the name of my company appeared multiple times over and over in the code. I'm pretty sure if I did that they'd be a tad upset.

Secondly, I know there are a lot of smart people at Google who come up with fancy mathematical equations. I wouldn't know how to read them even if they took them out of the highly secret drawer they keep them in and mailed me a copy to read at my leisure. Anyway, I have to believe that if they choose to they could find a way to discount anonymously posted content. We used to hang up on anonymous phone calls, so I don't know why Google allows credit to anonymous posters. I imagine they can also mathematically compensate for the element of human nature that has to click on something that points to something scandalous, even when the sentence doesn't make sense.

Recently Google has been rumored to be pushing more toward quality of rankings. Perhaps if one didn't have to page through bogus rubbish from a handful of anonymous people and companies with an advantage the rest of us can't compete with, Google's quality would be more like Bing's.

Google didn't say you shouldn't care about page 2 search results

"Most people only read Page 1 of Google results." "95% of people don't look past Page 1 of Google." Why do people in the reputation management and SEO business keep saying that?

Stop and think about it for a minute: There are plenty of people (professionals) who want us to believe the Holy Grail is somewhere on Page 1 of Google (above the fold, a very fashionable term). When it comes to reputation management the Search Engine Optimization (SEO), online marketers and reputation management professionals would keep us focused on Page 1 – "don't worry about Page 2; no one ever looks there!"

When it comes to products, services or anything else you are promoting I'd have to agree. Whatever is sitting on the cover gets seen first, right? Yep, until a negative link exists and then the rules change.

Whether it is 95%, 75% or 55%, I couldn't tell you what percentage of views on Google only go to Page 1. I don't know if it's an educated guess or an uneducated guess that people are perpetuating as fact.

If I'm looking to go to the movies I may type into Google "Fandango" and take a link on

Page 1 because the only reason I'm using Google for this search is because it requires a simple decision. No research required. The same thing is true of many, many convenience searches. We take a simple answer to a simple question. We even instinctively know we don't need to look further than Page 1 because our search term is clearly defined.

What about if the search is no longer a convenience search? Do we stop at Page 1 because it is too taxing to go to Page 2? Do we muster the energy to look at Page 3 when we are being asked to put trust into a decision? Yes, yes and yes. The more trust we have to commit to our own internal decision-making process, the further we go back and look.

What really happens to all those links that sit there on Page 2 through somewhere? Depending on the SEO tactics being used, what is the psychology at play and the intent of the host site? They can rise quickly. They can be the tsunami of links.

Strategies that fill up Page 1 of Google with meaningless junk don't solve reputation problems. It's not about having someone create page after page of meaningless directory pages with your company's name, address, phone number and a brief description. It's also not about paying bloggers to write some loosely connected stuff about us in broken English.

If it looks like a cheap suit it probably was a cheap suit – until we're dealing with reputation issues. Every mistake we make costs a fortune. The efforts we take to cover up a problem, to push down a problem listing, can in itself look, smell and feel like a complete cover-up. If we don't address the problem correctly, we just added to it.

We have to create the right content that serves a purpose other than trying to fill a spot on Page 1. Content and links created for the wrong purposes don't last. They rise and fall on Google like leaves from a tree. We continue to throw money at the same strategy until we realize our strategy was futile. Ding, ding, we have a winner – it's whoever we paid to implement the wrong strategy!

Chapter 7. Where reputation management problems start

Stop buying into all the hype about reputation management problems being an online problem requiring an online solution. Guess where that kind of talk comes from? The online industry! It represents half of the problem and half of the solution. The other half is firmly offline.

The online nature of the problem is a huge public spotlight on an age-old problem that existed well before anyone thought of the Internet, Google, Ripoff Report or any other type of complaint site.

Reputation problems are always human-driven. In a business environment we have owners, managers, employees, customers or clients and observers.

Owners: involved or not in the operations of the company are responsible for everything that happens. Involved or not they are responsible for the standards, ethics, pulse, quality and tone of the company. This relates to how the managers manage, how the employees act as employees, and how customers and clients act as customers and clients. Observers will be influenced by the impressions created by everyone else the owner is responsible for. So yes, the owner is also responsible for observers.

Managers are hired by owners. Managers hire managers. Good or bad the manager will operate within the standards allowable and acceptable. Acceptance is judged by allowance, not policy. The manager is responsible for carrying out his or her duties and responsibilities. Managers set the tone for the employees. The same employees that interact with customers and clients will influence the observer.

Employees are hired by managers. Employees carry out their duties and responsibilities not in accordance with policy, but according to what is considered allowable and acceptable by the managers, which they must then assume is ok with the ownership. A large number of employees behave according to their environment, and in the perceived vacuum of controlled standards they determine what is and is not acceptable when no one is looking.

Customers and clients have radar. Their first instinct is to figure out how you are going to wrong them. They have been trained to expect less and still they get surprised and upset when they get even less than they were told to expect. The problem is so many of us as consumers feel like we put our trust in someone or something every time we purchase or commit to something.

Your customers and clients are so used to getting less than they bargained for, that they try to remain indifferent to your product or service. How often do we say to ourselves when we get let down, "I knew it, I shouldn't have trusted them"?

We learned all of this from employees, managers and owners, right? As each of the above we train our customers and clients to think of us any way we choose. Have bad service once, and it may have been a bad day. Have a product fail unexpectedly, it may have been defective. What about when both scenarios continue? What if they are the norm? Who's to blame?

Look upwards not downwards!

Observers skim the headlines looking consciously or unconsciously for anything that stands out. They haven't had direct contact with your company. They may not know you exist nor need your product or service. Amongst the harmless observers that make up the bulk of the population are a small number of nasty observers.

The last thing you want to do is attract a nasty observer. Most observers have nothing to say about you or your company. They seek no pleasure from your pain. They have no axe to grind or financial profit to make. They just pass you by and that's good. The nasty observer always looks for something or someone to have fun with. Whether clinically, medically, emotionally or socially unstable, it's fair to say they will get pleasure from your pain.

What is the biggest problem facing a company's reputation? Every one of the groups listed above. Reputation management isn't an electronic or Internet problem; it's a human problem.

Your biggest problem when treated correctly also becomes your best defense against a reputation problem. When you have the ownership, managers, employees, and customers or clients in your corner your future looks bright. Everyone becomes part of a healthy immune system that can help fight off an attack.

What could have destroyed or severely damaged a company before can become an opportunity to validate the health and direction of the company based on the feedback you get. Build an offline defense, match it with an online strategy and reputation management is achievable.

Chapter 8. What you don't know might just kill your business

One of the first steps to figuring out the root cause of a reputation problem is understanding the dynamics of the employee base. What do they think of [the business]?

Most owners, CEOs and managers think they have a good feel for what employees think. The truth is they rarely do. Open communication is rarely open. Strings are always attached.

Put yourself in the employee's shoes for a minute. It's kind of a loaded scenario: *Do I look fat in these jeans?*

Most people take dare over truth when the real answer isn't good news. How many times does a manager or owner pull rank over the employee as justification for doing something a particular way?

Employees in far too many environments are trained for the most part to keep their heads down. "Dilbert" is funny because it made us recognize that we weren't the only ones. It was epidemic! *The Office* is a condensed look into the workplace. We all recognize the characters. We laugh because it shows the dysfunction of the workplace that we recognize.

Having an open, honest dialogue with employees will pinpoint problems quickly and efficiently. I can almost guarantee if I privately ask the owner to think like the employee and answer a series of questions as he or she thinks the employee would answer, the answers would be wrong half of the time.

That's a major disconnect which leaves an opening for a reputation management problem.

So how do you get an honest picture of what your employees are thinking or feeling?

Use an independent and objective employee survey source. Independence and objectivity are critical. If employees think their identity will be leaked, the results will be useless. Employees need to feel their input is important, that it will be treated with respect and that their identity will be kept confidential. How the questions are asked, and answer choices presented, can also influence the results.

The questions must be asked in a manner that does not create bias. The answer choices should not be strategically designed to create bias.

According to Dr. Jan Stringer, Ph.D., in a survey conducted by the California Job Journal, 73% of H.R. executives said poor leadership was the No. 1 cause for low employee morale, outnumbering workload and salary by a wide margin. And, in a report in Forbes magazine, 19,700 exit interviews revealed that 80% of employees left because of poor management or a "dysfunctional company culture."

The value of the responses will only be as good as the value of the survey or questionnaire. There is a right way to ask a question and there are better ways to ask questions. There are good ways and better ways to structure the answer choices. Employee surveys can be designed by experts specifically to find areas of concern.

For most companies, conducting an objective employee survey is the first step toward making changes. It alters the tone within an organization and gives ownership and management honest feedback. It becomes a foundation upon which to make changes. Employee surveys are not invasive or stressful. They are typically conducted via the Internet and require a minimum amount of time from the employee.

Always start at the beginning; define the real problem and go from there. A reputation doesn't have to be so difficult to manage.

Chapter 9. 10 ways to help avoid a reputation crisis

1. Do what you say you will

Whatever your product or service, deliver it above the expectations of your customer. At a minimum, you have to provide it as expected. If you are going to deliver something, deliver it on time. None of this should be hard to grasp; do to others as you want done for your mother.

2. Treat everyone with respect

Don't fight over something small. Winning shouldn't be what's important. Sometimes giving the appearance of losing a battle creates the best way to win the war. Knowing who's right and telling the other party they're wrong doesn't make for happy customers.

3. Be humble and apologize

Leave your ego at home and don't be afraid to apologize even when it's not asked for. Treat your customers better than they expect to be treated. Give them a reason to think of your company differently than they do of everyone else.

4. Treat your employees like you value them

If you want your customers to have a first-class experience, create a first-class environment for your employees. That means giving clear leadership they trust, respect that goes both ways, recognition to employees who deserve it, opportunity and incentive. I have met my fair share of business owners who believe giving their employee a paycheck means their responsibility to them is then complete.

5. Treat your employees like you value them

Am I making myself clear? Your employees can be the catalyst for a reputation nightmare or a reputation recovery. Employees who are not valued can passively and anonymously vent their frustrations online. One employee can cost you tens of thousands to millions of dollars in damages from lost revenues. Employees who do not feel valued will not provide anything more than the minimum experience needed to keep their job. That's a loss of revenue, customers, profit and reputation.

6. Only sell what you or your product can deliver

Why create a bad reputation by overselling a product or service capabilities? It makes no sense. You are asking for trouble. To make one sale you lose five. It's not just the customer who doesn't buy from you again that you lose. Lower expectations become lower credibility which becomes less service which deserves lower prices and lower margins.

7. Don't bait and switch or use bad sales tricks

Some of the oldest sales tricks in the book are just that – old sales tricks! Do you appreciate being or feeling tricked? Your customer doesn't appreciate it. Just like you and me, customers are tired of sales tricks and do everything to avoid the feeling. Most of us do what we can to avoid the bad sales tactics some people still insist on using. At the first sniff of a sales game you lose your credibility and a sale.

8. Give customers the real deal

Why mislead the customer? Whether it's in the terms and conditions or twenty pages of stuff no one reads, refund policies that don't allow for refunds, fine print that hides the real deal offered, or guarantees and warranties that aren't worth the paper they're written on. Don't mislead the customer.

9. Do something good in your community

To build the best reputation, you must do more than just provide good service and products. You have to care, and be known to care, about the community you live in and serve. Even if a person has no reason to connect to your product or service, there is no reason they shouldn't connect to your good deeds. Spread the joy; it isn't always money, sometimes it's time, manpower, resources or something that's worth a little to us and a lot to someone else. Give back to your community.

10. Don't think there are only ten things you can do to avoid a reputation crisis

There are hundreds of things we can all do to help avoid a reputation crisis. These are just ten. You should be able to think of a few of your own.

Chapter 10. You won't believe what's listed as the number 1 risk facing businesses globally today!

What's the number 1 risk facing businesses today?

Chief Reputation Strategist, Dr. Leslie Gaines-Ross of Weber Shandwick's global reputation consulting services and proprietary thought leadership development wrote,

> *"A sizeable 84% of global senior executives surveyed by the Economist Intelligence Unit reported that reputation risk increased significantly over the past five years. When executives were asked to choose among 13 risk types, reputation risk emerged as the most significant threat to global corporate business. Reputation risk exceeded all others, including regulatory risk, human capital risk, information technology (IT) network risk, and market risk. Reputation risk was considered even more threatening than terrorism, natural hazards, and physical security."*

Why reputation risk is considered the highest:

"Online scrutiny and exposure pose the greatest challenges for effectively managing company reputation in the future."

Online exposure is considered the greatest risk a business faces today – globally!

She's not talking about hacking; she's referring to the same reputation problems your business is exposed to every day.

So:

Do you wait until your brakes fail before you get them checked?

Do you look to see if you're in a flood plain after your home gets washed away?

Do you go to lock your car after it's been stolen?

Do you close your front door after you get burgled?

Do you cook the chicken after you get food poisoning?

Lack of online reputation management is the number one threat to businesses today and no business is exempt.

Some people skydive or get involved in adrenaline-pumping hobbies. Others leave themselves, their families, their employees and their families, and the communities they serve open to the risk of business failure, because reputation failure was simply never going to happen to them!

Good luck with that strategy!

Chapter 11. The most admired companies in America (And the world)

I read that Kim Harrison (www.cuttingedgepr.com) said the following:

A U.S. study showed there are ten main components of corporate reputation used in reputation measurement systems such as "The most admired companies in America":

1.   Ethical: the organization behaves ethically, is admirable, is worthy of respect, is trustworthy.

2.   Employees/workplace: the organization has talented employees, treats its people well, and is an appealing workplace.

3.   Financial performance: the organization is financially strong, has a record of profitability, and has growth prospects.

4.   Leadership: the organization is a leader rather than a follower; is innovative.

5.   Management: the organization is well managed, has high-quality management, and has a clear vision for the future.

6.   Social responsibility: the organization recognizes social responsibilities and supports good causes.

7.   Customer focus: the organization cares about customers; is strongly committed to customers.

8.   Quality: the organization offers high-quality products and services.

9.   Reliability: the organization stands behind its products and services, providing consistent service.

10.   Emotional appeal: it is an organization I feel good about; is kind, is fun.

Folks, it's not rocket science. If the list of 1 to 10 were discussing a business that's for sale, would it be at the low-value range or the high-value range? Any business that is described according to this list commands the highest value and is positioned to negotiate the best terms.

What about a business that models the opposite? It would have little to no current value and no control over terms if any were even offered.

So why make running a business difficult? It's easier to run a business when you are intent on being on the "most admired" list. Your revenue grows, your margins are healthy, your staff love going the extra mile for the company, and your customers look for ways to send you more business...

It's too hard!

It's too hard being less than you should be. It's hard not living up to the expectations you set. It's hard not being ethical, it's hard when your employees don't like coming to work, it's hard when you have to keep cutting to stay in business...

The companies striving for the "most admired" list are the companies that can rebound quickly from reputation challenges. Forgiven for an error, helped back on track. People *want* to see them overcome challenges.

The companies that strive for self are the companies that suffer greatly from reputation challenges. No one forgives their errors; they are forced deeper into a reputation challenge. People are willing to watch them fail.

It's never made any sense to me why some businesses struggle to understand the fundamentals. Doing things the right way with integrity and respect may not make you as rich as some, but it's a lot more rewarding than some of the other ways I've seen.

Most admired company in America and then the world. Aim high and make it fun – falling a little short is still a great place to be.

Chapter 12. Top 10 reputation management don'ts

1. Don't treat employees poorly

    Treating employees poorly will undoubtedly lead to a reputation problem. All that pent-up anger felt by the employee now has a very fertile market online. If you are like me you've probably said some things to someone when you were angry that you later wish you could take back. Online there is no taking it back. When the anger subsides, the once-angry employee or ex-employee's statements are typically etched in stone for all the world to see; and they're virtually permanent. Complaint sites don't take them down even when the employee asks them to.

2. Don't treat customers poorly

    If you don't think it's important to deliver a product or service to someone as it's expected to be, you will have trouble surviving in this new market of free and very public speech. You need to create an environment where your customer really does feel important to your business. Treat your customers poorly and not only do they take their money elsewhere, but they tell everyone why. Written in stone and it's not going away easily.

3. Don't threaten or agitate the host of a complaint site

Not that the host is going to do you any favors anyway. Your best strategy is to go unnoticed. Fly under the radar for as long as possible. Don't do anything to cause a person at the host site to focus specifically on you. In the early days of a posting or on a large and established complaint site, hundreds and possibly thousands of postings are made every day. Don't do something to stand out for the wrong reasons.

4. Don't join in an angry he said/she said online

You may not be able to defend yourself online, in an environment in which you are not well educated (Reputation Management). Trying to defend yourself against the wrong target in the wrong arena can lead to an onslaught of further negative postings.

5. Don't take the bait

And there will be plenty of it. Depending on the type of attack, you could be baited to join in the party online. It's like watching a bad horror movie; there's a noise coming from a room – you know you shouldn't go in there.

6. Don't bury your head in the sand

You can't do nothing, even if it seems to fly in the face of other "don'ts". There are plenty of things to do. Acting like it didn't happen is only going to make it worse. The damage is viral – it spreads online and offline. It can be slow at first but it's going to turn into an out-of-control machine that keeps spreading from site to site.

7. Don't buy someone's sales pitch

You are going to have to discuss your pain. It's going to make you dangerously susceptible to people that tell you they can make the pain go away. The solution isn't sitting in someone's proprietary system, software or iridescent warp drive convertor.

8. Don't fall for "do it now" and/or "trust me"

Come on, folks! If it sounds too good to be true it probably is. Be careful not to get distracted by statements that have little to do with what a company is doing or how they are doing it. Keeping the conversation on how great their company is such as "We're the biggest/best" might just be a well-implemented marketing strategy.

9. Don't think that any one expertise or company can defend or build your reputation; they can't!

Monitoring your reputation is not a defense. Monitoring your reputation is not a defense. Monitoring your reputation is not a defense. Say after me, "Monitoring your reputation is *not* a defense." You cannot solve a reputation problem, or potential problem, with Search Engine optimization (SEO), P.R., marketing, legal, business consultants, social media or reputation management companies working on their own. Reputation management is a multi-disciplined effort. It requires an orchestrated approach, using each element to a specific purpose and timing.

10. Don't go through this alone

No one has to go through this alone. Handling a reputation crisis is a difficult burden even for some broad shoulders. Even though the public denouncing of character, morals, ethics, and images of self that may be false, the shame that goes along with it is very real. It's not just owners who feel publicly demoralized by defamation online. Owners and their families, employees and their families, and customers all start to share in the feeling of shame by association.

Chapter 13. Want to know the answer to one of the most-asked questions of reputation management practitioners?

Should I respond to online criticism? This is one of the most consistent questions I get. There is a popular belief – supported by many in the reputation management industry – that you should never respond to online criticism. The established thought behind the response is that each posted comment adds credibility in the eyes of Google, which helps the string rank in the search engine. It keeps the string current and makes the posting more difficult to push down in the search results.

Valid point, but it's only from a single point of reference. If I'm the SEO guy or the normal reputation management guy I don't want anything making my job more difficult.

On the flipside, your customer base can take the absence of rebuttal as a sign of guilt! Not the intended result but still a common one. Left alone, the negative criticism can spiral out of control and once she's out of control she becomes a lynch mob.

There is a chance that when the response is crafted correctly early on in the life of the potentially growing string of negative comments, it can stop the criticism or at least slow it down and pause it.

More importantly, if the response is crafted correctly, your customers will see a valid attempt to address the comments.

The response should be a clean, simple attempt to establish a direct line of communication with someone in a position to meaningfully address the concerns. If someone has a concern, question or comment about X, a method of communicating should be provided that exists away from the string.

NEVER, EVER GET INTO A SQUABBLE, FIGHT, OR HISSY-FIT ONLINE!

Do not get pulled into a lynching. When responding to criticism online, you need to have eyes in the back of your head. It cannot be an emotional response.

You cannot win the battle fighting on someone else's turf. If they were there first it has become their ground.

Think about it this way: if I watch MSNBC it's probably because I share a similar philosophy with other people that watch MSNBC. The same is true if I watch Fox News. If I am of a different philosophy why would I expect a warm reception by airing my differing views on their turf?

Lynch mobs do not think and they don't care what the argument is about or how to get to neutral ground. They want to lynch someone and it may just as well be you if you make yourself available.

The lynch mob only has one objective; don't ever think they have two!

If you post a response there is always a chance you will be taunted and teased into coming back to the lynch mob – don't take the bait or you'll end up like an actor in a bad horror movie about to take an exit!

I have seen plenty of responses having the desired results, and I've seen plenty of people get lynched because they got sucked in.

Every situation is different and you have to look at everything in deciding your options. Don't throw out an option just because it's simple to go with "I wouldn't do it." Learn about all your options and make educated decisions.

Chapter 14. Getting the reputation you want

To start building the reputation you want, start creating your own PR, goodwill, publicity, information, and events.

Whether fighting for your reputation online or just building a good business, you have to create a positive perception of who you are and what you stand for.

Lose the hype, lose the sales pitch and start showing your community who you are and why they should be pleased to have you as a neighbor, even if they never need to speak to you.

Everything you do has the ability to be discussed or promoted to and by the community you want to influence online and offline; to past, present and future employees, customers, suppliers and passersby.

The world of media is now in everyone's hands and we have to start thinking of ways to use it to our advantage. What was just printed on hardcopy can now be made available online. Images can be added, video can be added, and presentations can be shown. Virtually anything can be shown online. We all have the power to be both publisher and editor of our own media.

My point is that if you've never done a customer appreciation event – do one. No matter how big or small – do it. You have an opportunity to create so much content. Words, still photography, video, customer testimonials, happy faces, positive press.

What about employee appreciation? It doesn't matter how big or how small the event. Think creatively. What do your employees want as recognition? It may not be what you think. Capture the essence of positive feedback and smiling faces. A picture of a smiling face says more than any mission statement.

Does your company give money, time, supplies or other items to various causes or charities? If so, you need to openly publicize your commitments. It doesn't matter if you're humble. Be humble with some of your charitable deeds and publicize the rest. Again, with so many media avenues available you have to start building the right image with every opportunity you have.

If you are not giving back and it doesn't have to be money, now is the time to start. I am a firm believer in creating good karma and what goes around comes around. Every company should give back to the community. It's just good business sense. The goodwill created by being involved can be huge. It is also great for morale. Get a group of employees to go to a local volunteer project and watch how they start to take more pride at work. Watch as the team strengthens and positive bonds are built. Watch how people start defending your reputation.

There are so many benefits to volunteering your time. It has to be one of the most meaningful, strongest ways to build a reputation. It shouldn't just apply to or include employees; it gets expanded to their families. So now there is a family and work bond being created between young and old – it can be great family time. Suppliers and customers can also get involved, strengthening bonds between everyone in the community.

Advertising isn't just about paid advertisements. The value of unpaid advertising can far surpass the return on paid advertising.

Reputation management is a continual process. Reputations are built and lost online and offline. We have the power to build strong reputations that everyone can be proud of. Once you decide what yours should look like you can set about achieving it. That's reputation management!

Chapter 15. Do your customers even like you?

Can you tell, or do you even care what they think? How do you know what they think about you?

Your reputation will help you attract or detract customers and clients. It's that simple. If you can't provide any intangible or tangible benefit to someone buying from your company, you become the lowest-priced provider. When you still fall below the level of service given by another low-priced provider you go out of business.

I used to hear from CEOs and owners that they couldn't possibly increase their prices to cover losses or break even. Their justification was always that someone else was already undercutting them. In virtually all cases, an example could be found of a company selling the same product or service that charged significantly higher prices, was profitable and stable.

Why? The level of customer satisfaction was higher. Customer satisfaction builds loyalty.

To create a solid defense against reputation problems, first know what your customers and clients think of you. You need to have strategies to strengthen your weaknesses. You have to learn how to collect, analyze, respond, adapt and use your customer feedback to build a positive reputation.

Fortune 100 companies have been studying and adapting their businesses to accept the voice of the customer for years.

Your customers and clients have been given their own front page to write whatever headline they want about you. If that doesn't scare you, it should! The only way you can minimize anyone's negative headline is by drowning it out amongst a number of others that say the opposite.

If the loudest headline is negative you have a major problem in attracting and keeping customers or clients. If the majority of headlines are negative you have a problem attracting and keeping customers and clients.

Here's the scary thing about math: one negative headline when there aren't any positive ones is one too many. Personally, I think you need at least twenty positives for each minor negative headline.

Your customers and clients are the ultimate trust-decider for prospects and continuing clients. Potential customers have no reason to trust the advertising pitch of the company and they have no reason to trust the employees; unless other customers say it's ok to trust.

If an existing customer had a less-than-favorable experience, they would be more likely to give you the chance to correct the mistake if the overwhelming support of the customer base says it's not the norm.

For any company to thrive in today's highly visible online world it has to learn how to harness the power of its customers' voices. Online customer reviews and surveys are a great tool to allow for maximum feedback. When you reach out to customers for genuine feedback, keep the questions or request simple and effective; make it non-intrusive.

If customers feel this isn't just another excuse to gather information about them, but a genuine opportunity to improve relations, products or service/s, you get the responses you need to build a solid defense.

Don't let one negative headline ruin your reputation, because you don't know how to capture views from the hundreds or thousands of already satisfied customers and clients you've helped along the way!

Chapter 16. Did customer service really die?

Search Google for "The Death of Customer Service" and it returns 170 million results.

Good customer service isn't dead but it sure is getting very difficult to find. Wherever you go, standards and expectations are being lowered. We all have plenty of experience with bad service or just no service. It's so commonplace that most of us don't do anything about it; we just keep doing what we do – giving abusers our money.

My daughter often questions me when I hold someone calmly accountable for it. "It's embarrassing, Dad!" What is? "You're always doing that stuff (she's smiling from ear-to-ear)." Lucky for me and my daughter we are both ok with me embarrassing her, especially when I have to remind people of common courtesies.

What if we get great or good service? Well, if you're anything like me, first, you're surprised, flabbergasted, and somewhat speechless. But then I have to shout it from the rooftops! Why? Because we don't openly do enough to support good service.

Do we in the moment reward the person for their effort? Do we make them feel good or do we take it for granted?

71

It's a little snobby of us to take it for granted. I love to reinforce great products and services with positive comments in the moment, or whenever the moment calls for it.

Businesses are failing everywhere for some really stupid reasons.

Owners and CEOs pay all kinds of experts to come in and solve their problems. As a business advisor, I always get a kick out of a CEO who tells me the economy is to blame for his declining or flat revenue stream.

Here's the truth – the tough love!

If your company's market share doesn't equal more than a substantial part of the market for your product or service, don't blame the economy. Your problems are internal not external. Even in a bad economy there is plenty of room for revenue growth – we just have to figure out how to do something better than our competition does.

It's too easy to blame the person you're dealing with for poor customer service or a poor product.

We even make excuses for them: "It's not their fault."

Consistently good or bad service stem from one place – ownership!

Ownership sets the tone for service. Ownership defines what's acceptable and what's not. Ownership puts in the management structure that hires, trains, and fires. Ownership sets the expectations for everything. Owners are kings and queens of their domain.

If owners want to influence their reputation, revenue and profit they'll eventually learn to take control of their customers' experience.

Chapter 17. What if reputation management companies were a scam, or fraud?

Here's what happens when you have an online reputation problem and you start looking for a quick fix: You are in so much pain that you are willing to take any pill that sounds about right. If it's affordable (at a stretch) and they seem confident in their abilities, you have everything to gain, right?

Wrong!

Slow down a bit. I know what I'm about to say doesn't reflect the intent of the whole "reputation management" industry, but it sure does represent a large portion of it. This is such a new branch of an online industry it has yet to really be defined. Reputation management in its current form is nothing more than an offshoot of the SEO business. If you're not careful, you'll fall prey to someone's sales pitch. You're an easy target to get something other than what you paid for.

I know I am going to take flak for this and I'm sorry if I offend good companies. From my own personal experience, this really is defining some of the self-professed main players who describe themselves as being in the reputation management business.

So many reputation management companies have already earned bad reputations; the allegations and negative comments show up within the first couple of pages of a Google search. How about they solve their own reputation problems successfully before claiming they have a solution for other companies?

When asked why they have negative results showing up about *them*, the response is typically defensive of how they became a target.

Ok, you're a target, I'm a target. I'm more interested in why the solution they promote will work for me but it doesn't work for them.

It's currently impossible to solve the problem to the degree it is being sold, using the solutions and strategies they use.

I have so many brightly colored proposals from a number of recognizable reputation management companies, all promoting some magical proprietary technology they've built.

I would so love to be wrong. I would love for it to be so simple. Audit, monitor, buy every domain name you can think of, open every social account you can think of...

Think of any celebrity or politician that has negative publicity. Then take a look at Google and look at the effect. Now ask yourself how much money they have spent with experts trying to change their online reputation.

One of my companies had been in the target's sights for years, dealing with what started as a single attack on Ripoff Report that turned into a nightmare. We had been in business for approximately fifteen years without blemish or concern, before one kid decided to write a few words on Ripoff Report. From that point on, we were the target of false, malicious attacks. The anonymous postings expanded from Ripoff Report to other sites as content got copied to other places just to start the attacks all over again.

I used "reputation management" companies in the past, in the problem's infancy. I remember thinking that at last someone gets it. It's obvious they understand the problem and I didn't have time to waste. I was on fire and they claimed to have water – *lots* of water!

Boy was I wrong! I never jumped at the first offer of a solution that came along. I went with what appeared to be the most credible. They said the right things and offered a level of confidence that basically said to me "problem solved".

For years I have talked to just about every major name that pops up when you search for reputation management companies, or other search concoctions that pinpoint someone who can fix a reputation problem. I have proposals from a number of them, including the "largest" and "best." I have made it a point to touch base with some of these companies from time to time to see what's changed.

It always makes me laugh when one of these companies that couldn't answer my simple questions before makes a follow-up call to me months later because they failed to update their records. I love questioning them about the guarantee they said they would send me the last time we spoke. It usually jolts them back to reality. I'll get called again a few months later though.

So here's what you need to be careful of:

The first thing you are going to discuss with a reputation management company is your problem. They will ask for your website address and a description of the problem. You can expect them to pull up a Google search of the problem term in order to understand the problem more clearly.

Here's the flipside of that: they are also looking for the pain – where can I find your buttons to make my sale. Remember you are dealing with a salesperson by any title looking to make a sale. You have to describe your problem honestly otherwise you stand no chance of getting the right solution. Makes sense!

You are likely to hear a description of what makes the reputation management company great. In one situation I was told, "We must be pretty good at what we do, we raised millions of dollars from a venture capital company; they wouldn't have given us the money if we didn't know what we were doing." Stop! Don't get distracted, it's a magic trick and we are being distracted, watching the left hand, while we should be watching the right hand.

I have also been told how the reputation management company has been on various news channels and referred to by the media. Ok, some of the media that looks like news is actually a paid spot. It's made to look like news but it's really just an advertisement. There's nothing wrong with this approach. It's perfectly legitimate but you have to put things in perspective.

A good PR company and a budget can get you in front of media channels. Be it television, cable, print or online. Again, there's nothing wrong with having a good PR approach (I wish there were more of them), but don't let the spin cloud your vision. Don't be fooled by the flashy trim. It's another magic trick meant to distract you.

Tell me how this works. How do you make my problem go away? I don't care how you ask the question but you need to run for the hills when you hear something that sounds too simple or too good to be true. You have to be able to understand the basic logic behind the strategy; if you don't get it, find someone that should.

Don't accept "We spent millions of dollars developing software, a proprietary system" that basically they can't or won't discuss. Are we asking to see the source code? I didn't think so. I've been told, "Trust me, we wouldn't have spent so much building it if it wouldn't work."

Beware of the Trekkie talk; the hyper-dynamic cross-functional linking tool that plugs into the third warp is really what makes us better than anyone else. Oh, that's what it is! Well then please take my money.

Beware of any form of guarantee. I can't say it any better than this taken from the movie *Tommy Boy*:

<u>Tommy</u>: Let's think about this for a sec, Ted. Why would somebody put a guarantee on a box? Hmmm, very interesting.
<u>Ted Nelson, Customer</u>: Go on, I'm listening.
<u>Tommy</u>: Here's the way I see it, Ted. Guy puts a

fancy guarantee on a box 'cause he wants you to feel all warm and toasty inside.

Ted Nelson, Customer: Yeah, makes a man feel good.

Tommy: 'Course it does. Why shouldn't it? Ya figure you put that little box under your pillow at night, the Guarantee Fairy might come by and leave a quarter. Am I right, Ted?

Ted Nelson, Customer: What's your point?

Tommy: The point is, how do you know the fairy isn't a crazy glue sniffer? "Building model airplanes," says the little fairy; well, we're not buying it. He sneaks into your house once, that's all it takes. The next thing you know, there's money missing off the dresser, and your daughter's knocked up. I've seen it a hundred times.

Ted Nelson, Customer: But why do they put a guarantee on the box?

Tommy: Because they know all they sold ya was a guaranteed piece of xxxx. That's all it is, isn't it? Hey, if you want me to take a dump in a box and mark it guaranteed, I will.

Folks, I've yet to see a guarantee that was the guarantee you thought you had. There is always an out. It is impossible and if not illegal it's unethical to guarantee the actions of a third party (person or company) because you can't control what they will do.

Think about it for a moment. Google's algorithms are well-documented as being secret. Google continually changes them. How can you guarantee something today that you have no control over tomorrow? You can't, folks!

I have been offered a few guarantees from reputation management companies over the years; however, they seem to disappear when I question the exact nature of the guarantee. So many of the responses come down to "trust me".

I actually did manage to talk my way into getting information from one of the top reputation management companies. They gave me a screen shot of a company with various language removed to hide the name. I was given it so I could see the "quality of the content they produce." I wrote a couple of lines from the screen shot into Google and – bingo – up pops a dentist's website! Funny, it was the same dentist the same company provided me with years earlier. I was told this was a "new client project" and it was the sales guy's "personal client that he had talked to about getting permission to share the screen shot."

When the sales guy called me back to see if I'd gotten the email with the screen shot, he was speechless when I gave him the dentist's name and pointed out all the reputation problems that still existed on Google for this guy. He failed to explain how this was the same guy I'd been pointed to about three years prior.

Here's a simple question that seems to stump any reputation management company that suffers its own reputation problem: why can't you remove or push down (however they refer to it) the site that presents negative info about your own company on Page 1 of Google?

I've heard, "What site? It must have just appeared and we haven't been paying attention; you must have done something by mistake on your end – I don't see it, we'll get rid of it in a couple of days."

A couple of days after they cash my check! How about you get rid of it and then call me about *getting* a check?

I've also had the guy on the phone try to get me to sign a contract before he has to take that "very important scheduled meeting with a wealthy businessman in London and he would love to get things started before he leaves for a couple of weeks." They've told me they work with so many high-profile, celebrity clients – they just can't tell me who they are! It's confidential, you know!

Reputation management companies move quickly to get you signed up. Makes sense, right?

You have a major problem and they want to fix it for you quickly!

I've got a better understanding:

How about this one: they are in a competitive environment where the barriers to entry are low – anyone can become a reputation management company. Your solutions are mostly based on a sales pitch and the profit margins can be huge.

Now, you tell me why it's important that they sign you up quickly?

Beware when you get told we can remove postings.

'Remove' may have a whole new definition than the one we grew up with. The reputation management companies have no control over the site that hosts the information, unless of course they own the site that hosts the information. That's a novel thought!

The law as stated within the Telecommunications Act of 1996, Sec 230 basically protects the host site and creates a level of defense against prosecution that is virtually impenetrable. Maybe the host site has a soft spot for reputation management companies that I don't understand. Please let me know if you understand how they can remove a posting – just because.

Posting and information on the web is viral in nature, which basically means that while information may not show up over here anymore it may still show up over there, and then over there and so on.

Pushing down a site. It's the basic strategy of reputation management. Terrific! But not the way they may sell it to you. In order to push something down, you have to create more stuff on top. How does stuff such as sites or content stay on top? Well Google hasn't exactly made that clear to anyone. That's what everyone is trying to figure out. It's the holy grail of the Internet. And just when we think we've figured it out, Google changes a few things to upset the balance again. They even have rules about what you can't do.

What you can't do: Google and others split the tactics used to manipulate search rankings into two categories; black hat – what you are not allowed to do, and white hat – what you are allowed to do.

Google is good enough to make it clear about what you can't do. Ask Matt Cutts at Google and I'm sure he can point you in the right direction. If your site or sites are ranking because of black hat tactics, expect Google to take your site down. That means turning the lights out on your site while leaving the others shining brighter than ever.

How long does a site go dark for? Ask Google! Some reputation management companies may run some extremely questionable strategies. It's not their site that goes dark first, it's yours. Google may out them but that won't help you.

One strategy is to create links to other sites. You may get sold on the number of links a reputation management company will create. Links are not created equal. Links change over time. Links have different values. You may have a thousand links created for you that do not equal the value of the one that's hurting you.

Link values change over time. In one sense, as the Internet is alive – so is each link. There is no one-month, six-month, or twelve-month strategy. It's a lifetime strategy.

Content creation is another tool. New, fresh and relevant sites and content are important. So you hire a reputation management company that creates content and sites for you. They submit your stuff to all kinds of directories. They are even good enough to create tens of sites that just have your name and address on them. First of all the content may be written in broken English – I've seen it from the most respected names. Secondly, it can be so off-target that it creates an online credibility problem. It can be posted on sites that have absolutely nothing to do with your business. Even when done correctly, content creation is an ongoing strategy. It's not something that only gets done for six months.

You probably wouldn't let just anyone hand-paint your business name on the front door with a 4-inch brush so why do it with your content? Content really is king!

Here's a word or two: Google is taking steps to devalue sites that are created for the purposes of simply occupying space. Why? When a study was done that included quality of search return numbers for Bing and Google, Google was not where it wanted to be. If I remember correctly Bing delivered a higher percentage of relevant search returns. That's a problem for Google and they're not letting it slide. Search relevance is what keeps us going back to a search engine.

Are there things that good reputation management companies bring to the table? Yes. Being focused on one area of the online industry should bring about new strategies and discussions. I have nothing against good companies being profitable, making a buck or getting paid for providing a valuable service.

My dissatisfaction with the reputation management industry of today is that for too many it appears to be about making a fast buck, based on a sales pitch aimed at a client who will do and believe anything to make his or her pain go away.

Ultimately, reputation management is a virgin industry or solution. Furthermore, current reputation management solutions do not address the actual problem; they simply try to cover it up. In every situation, I found when looking into the patterns and strategies around reputation management companies that included looking at the paid bloggers and writers they use, I was able to find a number of their clients who still had a reputation problem.

Far too many reputation management companies need to reign in their sales tactics. Truth in advertising may not apply but ethics always do.

When dealing with reputation management issues we (practitioners) don't have too many opportunities to get the answer wrong, and need to hold our fiduciary responsibilities to a higher standard.

Reputation management needs specific expertise involved in various phases of both online and offline solutions. Covering up the problem is not a solution. If your idea of reputation management is to sweep the problem under the proverbial rug, you're going to need a lot of rugs. It keeps coming back – over and over! Understand what's causing the problem, then go fix it.

Chapter 18. Search engine optimization (SEO), can it solve my reputation problem?

The simple answer is no, it can't! Search Engine Optimization or SEO, as it is commonly referred to, is a much-needed component of reputation management – but it is not *the solution*.

Per Wikipedia: "Search engine optimization (SEO) is the process of improving the visibility of a website or a web page in search engines via the 'natural' or unpaid ('organic' or 'algorithmic') search results."

And for most of us that really means it's how we improve the chances of a website being seen when someone performs a search using a search engine.

SEO as a strategy takes into account what people are searching for, the guidelines provided by the search engines, linking strategies and search terms. Optimizers work with the computer code and content to increase the site's relevance to specific keywords, and to remove barriers to the indexing activities of search engines.

Huh?

SEO strategy tries to get that thing you want to get in front of an online audience, in front of an online audience.

A good SEO company will keep you squarely out of trouble with the search engine police by using only white hat techniques. A second type of strategy is described as black hat. You need to stay away from black hat. It may sound good while you're in pain, but before you know it your quick fix just blew your site right off the web. If you are found using black hat techniques, the search engine will technically turn the lights out on your site or at least make sure no one finds your site through their search engine.

Again, as Wikipedia puts it: "Black hat SEO or spamdexing, uses methods such as link farms, keyword stuffing and article spinning that degrade both the relevance of search results and the quality of user experience with search engines. Search engines look for sites that employ these techniques in order to remove them from their indices." Why am I dwelling on black hat? Because just like opium, black hat can be packaged up and sold to anyone who needs the pain to go away.

Again, there are good SEO companies that do good SEO work. But SEO is only a *component* of reputation management, not the reputation solution. So what's the problem with SEO or SEO companies? To put it bluntly, they seem to think they are the solution!

I have used a number of SEO companies over the years and I've talked to many, many more. The first SEO company I used assured me they could remove/push down Ripoff Report; plenty of others have made similar statements about copycat sites. Initially, some SEO companies got to me as I didn't know any better when I started dealing with these online problems, and I honestly don't think they knew any better either at the time. This was all breaking new ground.

The SEO companies were always quick to point out when their strategy didn't work that you just have to give it more time. Time was always, always, being sold to me at a cost to me and a benefit to the SEO company. The trouble is, and still appears to be, a consistent story that time runs out and if you just continue to pay monthly for longer than you originally expected to – based on the SEO company's original opinion – the strategies will work. At least that's what I'm told!

I understand the benefit SEO strategies create. Here are the real issues I have with SEO companies: for one, it's a mindset, a mental thing. SEO companies don't understand reputation problems. Yes, just like looking at someone with a gash in their knee they can see that it hurts. They can understand that it hurts. They can't seem to feel just how bad it is. They don't seem to understand that the gash goes all the way to the bone and if you don't get it fixed soon you're going to lose the leg.

So SEO companies can end up putting together what would be fabulous strategies to increase your brand awareness online. They can do wonderful things to raise your chosen search terms against your competitors. They can tell you where and how to initiate a pay-per-click campaign that suits your goals of market awareness and ROI from that awareness. But SEO as part of reputation management is a different animal. It takes a certain level of understanding of your opponents. A good SEO company has to roll up its sleeves and get its hands dirty.

On the other side of this problem is an SEO guy somewhere who plays by a different set of rules than the ones we are used to. He's also got the law and human nature giving him an advantage. Eventually your SEO guy will tell you when things aren't going as planned, "I can't do what they do".

There really are good SEO companies out there. They have some of the skills needed to solve part of the reputation management problem. But if you hire an SEO company to do reputation management, don't be surprised if they just relabeled their services and charged you extra because in the world of reputation management the removal of emotional pain is something most of us are willing to do at any cost.

Chapter 19. Search engine optimization (SEO) is great, but it's not reputation management

Let's break down the SEO jargon someone will try to get you to buy, in order to fix a reputation management problem.

If you are like me, at least initially, SEO was a technical term I'd heard but hadn't figured out what it meant yet. It seemed every time I tried to have someone break it down for me I was given another layer of technical jargon.

SEO was something everyone kept telling me I needed to fix my problem, but no one could ever explain *how* it could fix my problem.

There are brilliant SEO people working within the SEO industry, doing brilliant things. They must be just as ticked off as I am at companies with little SEO experience claiming to be SEO experts.

Have you ever seen the guy with 3 small cups, hide a ball under a cup, only to then ask you to guess which cup the ball

is under. I know you think you've got it – but you don't. Try again as the cups move around. What about this time? Nope!

The problem with SEO is that it is a discipline that exists to increase paid or organic visibility of keywords. That's different from reputation management.

What does that mean? In most situations let's say you wanted your website or page of something (we'll call that a link) to show up when someone types "fairy dust" into a search engine (say Google) search box. You would legitimately have a need for SEO services. Their job would normally be to get your link showing up as high as possible on the search terms.

Don't fall for claims of "We got our client to the top spot of Google, blah, blah, blah…. It might have been for the specific or exact spelling of the company name or some strange acronym. It could, to put it another way, be for something no one else wanted or searched for.

Here's the problem with just looking at how to raise a link or two up on Google: You potentially have – and Google changes this from time to time – about twelve spots on Page 1 (let's not worry about Page 2 until you've mastered Page 1). Some of those potential negative links that show up when someone searches your name may have thousands and thousands of links attached to their page.

I know some links or other pages attached (think about a chain) may not be as credible, and

94

I'm told Google will assign a weighting factor to the link to straighten out their value – it really doesn't matter. Imagine if you wanted to compete with IBM for space on a search engine result just by using SEO strategies. It would take major effort, time and money to start seeing the smallest benefit.

The SEO company will tell you they are doing good work: "We were able to move from spot 129 to 57." Possibly putting your page on Google's Page 5. While this is happening you are getting killed on Page 1.

"Keyword research," the SEO people shout as being the salvation. Terrific!

It's the foundation of good SEO, they say. Start putting a list of your services or words that might be important to you together. Then the good SEO company will put them into a piece of software and generate a whole bunch of sounds like, or if it was misspelled it could be this. All good if you are trying to capture more of an audience – more traffic. SEO people are focused on, and understand how to talk traffic.

You don't need to talk about getting more traffic – you are in a war and it's your reputation and business you're fighting for. There is no time for the SEO company to move the cup or the ball.

What about content editing? Absolutely! Have an SEO company or someone else with the skill-set go through your website and make sure it is, at a minimum, optimized. Have them go through the page titles, meta descriptions, headline texts and page elements. They should be making sure your site is easily read (crawled) by the search engines. There are no secrets here – just good SEO business practices. Don't try to learn about crawls, bots and spiders or you'll see the cup move but lose the ball.

SEO companies love to spread the work out on a retainer for six to twelve months. However, it doesn't take that much time or work to research and implement the initial SEO work.

Inbound links: Here's where it gets tricky. You always know you are getting closer to the thing no one wants you to see because they guard it. Search engines like Google guards what you can and can't do with inbound links. They make no bones about it – if you get too close to the line they will stop you (take your site down).

The trouble is this is like dealing with the IRS. There are thousands of pages of rules. Most are not fully understood by the average CPA. Some CPAs live in the grey area between black and white. Some are ultra-conservative and some are overly aggressive in their interpretation of the rules. Which one is right for you? For me it's the one who studies everything in relation more than the others, and is therefore able to predict where the line is and walks right up to it, but doesn't cross it.

Link-building seems to be a key driver to how things rank. There appears to be within the SEO community a number of different opinions as to where the line is that you shouldn't cross. Maybe it's because Google doesn't make it clear where the line is, and then moves it as people get close to figuring it out. I don't know.

I am convinced that there is a link-building expertise being defined and separated from within the SEO world that will purely develop link strategy.

Don't fall for the SEO pitch of "We will submit a minimum of X inbound links per month to our proprietary link list. It sounds great. X times the number of months you retain them for equals Y, right? Wrong!

It means they will send out requests for links. It doesn't mean anyone is going to say – link away!

A few months into your SEO contract, the SEO company will now add the caveat "It takes time to see the results from their link submissions". Just how much time seems to be a difficult question to get an answer to.

We can set up social media profiles for you. Ok. Depending on your level of comfort in dealing with social media such as Facebook, Twitter, LinkedIn, Flickr, Slideshare, Google Plus, YouTube and others, you may want to use an SEO company to help you maximize the benefit of these. Don't confuse setting up social media profiles with ongoing SEO work – they are not the same!

There is a ton of information available online about setting up and using social media for business. If you can't handle this level of setup and support find someone that can.

Don't allow it to be sold as part of your six- to twelve-month SEO bundle. Yes, it helps with SEO, but once set up it becomes more about PR and marketing.

SEO is an absolute necessity to being online. You can't live without it as part of your online strategy. It reaches legitimately into areas of pay-per-click (PPC), CPI, CPM and a bunch of other acronyms surrounding the business of paid online advertising.

I am not faulting good SEO strategy. Just remember: it is not all-encompassing.

Chapter 20. Should I use a public relations or marketing company to help with my reputation problem?

If you don't know the difference between a political and traditional PR model – you might just buy a lemon!

Major PR/marketing companies have crisis management teams and strategies. I'm not sure they've been reserved for small business though. If it's a regular PR company, you will probably have to train them on how to help you with your problem, using their tools.

In talking to many PR and marketing companies about a reputation problem online, I discovered they were out of their comfort zone. This is not a traditional PR problem. Even when talking to a crisis management team from one of the most respected names in the PR world, I found myself first having to explain the basics of who the online players were, what their apparent motives were and how everything around Sec 230 worked.

The questions they asked clearly showed a lack of understanding of the complexities of the problem. It didn't take long to realize we both knew traditional PR companies weren't the way to go.

I ran into a lot of PR and marketing companies more interested in the normal components of a professional relationship. Shaping product and service rollouts and whitepapers is far different than dealing with a malicious attacker with an unknown identity.

I found it interesting too that PR and marketing companies – even ones that listed reputation management/crisis management as a service – really didn't understand reputation management and were quick to run away from the problem. The same is true of PR companies that claim crisis management as a skill-set – more of an exaggeration.

There is no question that PR and marketing companies can do great work, but when it comes to reputation management you need to be the leader in guiding where their expertise is best applied.

You don't have the luxury of a traditional PR or marketing approach. You need a message now! You need to find a voice and a place to be heard. You don't need the PR company to shape replies to malicious criticism and you don't need to speak through a PR or marketing machine. It's time to make an impact on your reputation – fast! It may be that you're spending too much time looking for the proverbial needle in the haystack!

Chapter 21. Will suing Ripoff Report or a growing list of copycat sites get a negative comment removed?

Probably not! If you're thinking of suing an online company because of comments you consider damaging, you and your attorney need to come to grips with the Telecommunications Act of 1996, Title V, commonly called the Communications Decency Act of 1996, Sec 230. Once you've done that, ask yourself: Am I ready for the fight of my life? How much money am I willing to throw at it and how long can I continue to throw money at it?

Was I ready for the fight of my life?

I walked in these shoes. We knew nothing of the laws and thought only of justice (it sounds so cheap when you find out what justice is). We spent a considerable amount of money exploring legal solutions to the problem of anonymous, false and malicious online criticism. We believed the courts and laws must be on our side because we were innocent. How could the law be on the side of someone who makes false statements about you? You have no idea how quickly a corporate attorney can suck $200,000 out of your coffers because of your pride, ego and naiveté.

If we've never needed justice, we are left to falsely believe in the romantic notion that justice gives us protection or accountability for an injustice. It makes us all sleep better! Justice and the law have very little to do with each other in the real world. For example, if someone says you have a criminal record, it doesn't take an attorney long to substantiate the facts on this one. You either do or you don't have a record.

When it comes to defamation, the truth – as shameless as this sounds – is that it's nowhere close to what you thought it was. "They cheat, lie, scam"! Here's what these points came down to: it's not whether we/you cheated, lied or scammed in a specific moment. It's whether you ever cheated, lied or scammed in your life. How can you prove you've never lied, cheated, or scammed at any time in your entire life? If we can't prove that we didn't, it's possible we could have cheated, lied or scammed at some time in our lives, and therefore we have no claim against defamation for being falsely accused of cheating, lying or scamming in the broad sense. It would have been an impossible task for Mother Teresa to meet the legal requirement.

You're probably thinking, *Bulls..t!* So, wait until your attorney is arguing in front of a pro bono corporate lawyer (et al) who represents 60,000 free speech defenders. They'll show you how to spend money defending your legal arguments. And you'll be left in the corner with nothing when they're through!

Defamation was not what we thought it was. You end up with judges favorable to certain whims and opinions; federal court is good for this, but state court is good for that. And even if you make it to step one, and find out the identity of the anonymous person maliciously posting about you, that still doesn't mean any postings come down.

Even if the person responsible for making false allegations says their comments were false, that *still* doesn't mean the comments come down!

You have the difficult task of finding a way through the protections afforded within Sec 230 of the Communications Decency Act of 1996. You *may* be able to find the individual who posted the information if – and it's a big "if" – the hosting site captures the IP address (the address the posting came from), and the anonymous poster was stupid enough to post from a computer that can be traced to an IP address with their name on it. "If" is going to be a very expense game to play. If you do find the individual and can prove he or she was responsible, you could take them to civil court and win damages. And if they are wealthy enough you might actually get five bucks a month for the rest of your life.

In reality if you win damages against a person you may have judgments against someone for the rest of their life in order to collect or attempt to collect on the judgment. I'm all for holding someone accountable and for receiving damages but, don't cut off your nose to spite your face. It won't get you your reputation back. I've won judgments against people – deservedly. I still never received a penny. What I got was another request from the attorney to go back to court and an invoice for their time.

We've all seen a high-profile trial on TV. Remember how the attorney for the other side did everything to destroy the opponent's credibility? You will not believe the negative publicity or spin that will be added to your reputation problem by even more "anonymous" parties. The spin is going to show up anywhere their attorney can get it.

If you thought you had a problem before, it may have just been an itch compared to the problem you have now. This has nothing to do with whom or what's right; it has everything to do with the court of public opinion, and you lose there before you ever get to a courtroom.

Remember the lawyer that defends the other party is a pro at making you look bad. I don't blame them; it's their job to defend their client. Be prepared for a further deluge of postings on all kinds of sites about how you are trying to squash the freedom of speech, and how you – the bad guy – simply don't like being criticized, and respond by taking little guys to court.

It's really brilliant how a good attorney can win out of court by adding more of the same false stuff. *Lots* of stuff!

Because this topic sails close to some very heated topics of conversation, you can attract some really powerful representation working against you on a pro bono basis. Freedom of speech is a high-profile fight and that's what it will get turned into – at least in the public eye.

I can't tell you not to sue someone as I may get sued for giving legal advice and to be clear, I'm not an attorney!

The legal and philosophical arguments around the Communications Decency Act of 1996, Sec 230, are far more complex than the majority of us take into account. The lessons I learned from going through the legal battle were worth every penny. It reaffirms that life isn't fair even when you think there's this thing called justice, which is supposed to protect us and help us sleep better at night.

Before you go filing a lawsuit against someone or staying angry about what's not fair, I suggest you read everything you can about the issues surrounding Sec 230 and freedom of speech as it relates to the same.

You need good attorneys so don't take what I'm about to say the wrong way; if you ask an attorney if you should sue someone, you're asking a person who makes their living from suing someone if you should buy his product!

Most attorneys are going to get paid whether they win or lose for you, so in the words of an attorney, *caveat emptor* – buyer beware!

He or she knows only too well that they can't give you a guarantee, and because it's a supposedly respected profession you accept their wisdom, opinion and pleasantly positive outlook for going forward with the case. That's all the convincing you need to take your money out of your pocket and sign it over to the attorney. You found a place to vent your anger and your attorney is going to help you show everyone that you're not to be pushed around.

Quit being angry and start looking at the problem – and the solution –differently.

I've spent years contemplating the Communications Decency Act of 1996. I'm not suggesting I'm any smarter than the next guy or more or less capable than the next person when it comes to figuring out the nuances involved in deciding freedom of speech issues.

I believe it is pretty widely accepted that changes need to be made to the Communications Decency Act of 1996 or at least to Sec 230 of Title V of the Act. It might be even fairer to say that a growing number of people recognize the Act has inadequacies, that it's not perfect. I don't think anyone knows how to – or what – to change, if anything.

I also think freedom of speech is something that needs to be protected. I can guarantee you that means I'll get offended and sometimes repulsed by what some people have to say. But, I'd still rather live in a place that allows them to say it.

It may not be as black-and-white as we think and as my grandmother used to say, "You'd better be careful what you wish for, my boy."

She was one smart Welsh woman!

Chapter 22. The grand poobah of complaint sites is www.Ripoffreport.com

With an estimated monthly SEO traffic value in the hundreds of thousands of dollars, it's easy to see why the site exists. The number of pages indexed by Google is estimated at over several hundred thousand. This makes this site a monster in the rankings. The remaining portion of this chapter is taken directly from www.Ripoffreport.com. Once you finish reading it all (if you can make it), you'll understand why the level of intimidation and confusion is so high. Chapter 23 will help to put things in perspective.

I did not write the rest of this chapter. This is all in their own words. I'm including this so that you get a real sense of their opinion:

Want to sue Ripoff Report?

Do you have any of the following questions?

•There's a false report about me on this site!!! What can I do?

•If my lawyer sends you a threatening letter, will you remove the report?

•I heard that Ripoff Report has been sued many times and has never lost a case. Is that true?

•I heard Ripoff Report has a NEW arbitration program which can result in false statements being removed. Is that true?

•If you answered 'YES' to any of these questions, please read this information before filing a lawsuit against Ripoff Report or its founder, Ed Magedson.

TABLE OF CONTENTS (This is all in their own words)

7. What if the original author asks us to remove a report?

8. Specific Answers To Frequently Asked Questions

•If I get the original author of a report to send a retraction demand, will Ripoff Report remove the complaint?

•My lawyer says you have to remove false information upon demand, is that true?

•My lawyer says Ripoff Report has to verify complaints before they are posted and I can sue if you don't, is that true?

•Someone posted a report which violates Ripoff Report's Terms of Service. Will you remove it?

•If I file a lawsuit against Ripoff Report, will that get my complaint removed?

•I heard that Ripoff Report pays Google to get higher rankings in search results, is that true?

•Other websites have said that Ed Magedson writes reports and titles to reports, is that true?

•I want the name of someone who posted an anonymous report about me. How can I get that?

•I Heard That Ripoff Report Is An Extortion Scheme; What's Up With That?

•I Know the CDA Protects Ripoff Report, But I Am Going to Sue Anyway!

1. Introduction

From time to time, Ripoff Report receives notices from companies and individuals who claim that false or inaccurate information about them has been posted on this site. Sometimes we receive letters from lawyers with similar allegations. These people sometimes threaten to sue Ripoff Report unless the statements they do not like are removed.

If you are considering sending us a notice or demand (or if you have already done so), this page is intended to provide you with information that may help you to better understand the situation and your rights, as well as the rights of the people who post reports here. You need to understand that threats against Ripoff Report are not effective, nor will they result in the removal of any reports. Here's why.

2. Our Policy: Why We Don't Remove Reports

Since Ripoff Report was started in 1998, our policy has always remained the same – we don't remove reports. We will not remove reports even when they are claimed to contain defamatory statements. We will not remove reports even if the original author asks us to do so. Also, contrary to what our critics would like to believe, we will NOT remove reports for money. Don't believe us? Just make us an offer and see how we respond.

Some people have criticized this policy as being unfair, but we strongly feel this policy is essential, fair, and far better than the alternative – rampant censorship.

We have many reasons for our policy, but here are three of the most important ones:

FIRST – we are not in a position to judge the credibility and truthfulness of the 600,000+ reports and the many millions of other comments posted on our site. Except for statements clearly marked as "Editor's Comments" (or otherwise indicated as being from us), all material posted on Ripoff Report is created entirely by third-party users of our site, not by us (this includes reports AND their titles). Because our reports come from users, we are not in a position to know what is accurate and what isn't. Of course, when people contact us to dispute the accuracy of something on our site, we have no way of knowing who they are or whether they are telling the truth. For that reason, we cannot simply remove reports because one side claims that something in the report is inaccurate. Taking sides is not our role.

This position isn't unusual. Consider these examples: Facebook does not fact-check the accuracy of every post from all of its 500+ million users. Amazon.com doesn't verify the accuracy of all its user reviews, nor does Twitter confirm that every tweet is 100% true. Just like these sites, Ripoff Report cannot and does not investigate the accuracy of everything posted by our users. For any website that allows user-generated comments, investigating and verifying every posting would be economically and practically impossible, so the law (at least here in the United States) does not hold website operators responsible for the accuracy of material posted by a user.

SECOND – we do not remove reports because we believe this site is most effective when all complaints are maintained and preserved so that over time patterns of truly bad business practices are exposed. If we removed reports upon request or after a certain period of time, this would provide consumers with less information to use when evaluating a company. Unlike the Better Business Bureau (which deletes complaints after just 36 months and which has been accused of hiding complaints in exchange for money), we maintain a permanent record of all complaints. This ensures that our viewers have more information rather than less.

THIRD – if we removed complaints on request this would give companies an incentive to pressure authors to remove true and accurate reports in exchange for money or simply to avoid a costly lawsuit. It's a well-known fact that most people aren't willing or able to spend $100,000 in legal fees defending a defamation lawsuit, so even when a person has written a 100% true report, there is a huge amount of pressure for them to just remove it when threatened with legal action.

For that reason, we will not agree to remove reports upon request, even if someone can show that a report is probably inaccurate. By having this policy, we take leverage away from companies who threaten or pressure a customer hoping to get them to retract a valid complaint.

If this seems unfair or unreasonable, consider this: if someone sues you in court and makes outlandish claims that are completely false, you can fight the case and win and at the end a judgment will be entered in your favor proving that you were right and your accuser was wrong. However, the court clerk will NOT destroy the file or seal the records of the case simply because you won. Even when a lawsuit is shown to be 100% baseless, the documents remain part of a public record that is maintained for years or perhaps forever (trust us – we KNOW about this from first-hand experience). In this situation, the remedy you are entitled to is a court order or judgment proving that you were right, not the destruction of public records about the case.

3. NEW – Does Ripoff Report Offer Any Alternatives For Dealing With False Statements? YES!

As explained above, Ripoff Report has always had a strict no-removal policy, and we have spent millions of dollars in legal fees over the years defending that policy. To date, every court that has ever considered the merits of our policy has found it to be entirely lawful. For many years, this meant that companies or individuals who were unhappy about something posted on our site had essentially no recourse against us (the law has always allowed victims to pursue the original author of a false statement, but not the website host).

Understandably, this resulted in a lot of frustration for people who felt victimized by something on our site. Individuals who wanted to dispute the accuracy of something posted on our site had only one option – hire a lawyer to pursue the author through the civil court system. Of course, lawsuits can take years to resolve and even reasonably priced lawyers can cost $100,000 or more. This made litigation an impossible option for a large number of people. It also made Ripoff Report the target of a lot of criticism because we did not give people any other options for dealing with inaccurate reports.

Well, GOOD NEWS – things have changed. In response to overwhelming demand for a cheaper, faster, and easier alternative to litigation, Ripoff Report recently launched a new program which we call V.I.P. Arbitration. This program allows anyone to dispute the accuracy of any facts in a report (because there's no such thing as a false opinion, only facts can be disputed in our program, not opinions).

How does this program work? It's very simple, and it's designed to be non-technical and easy to understand so that you don't need to hire a lawyer to participate, though you are allowed to do so if you wish.

If you feel that a report on our site contains a false statement of fact that you'd like to dispute, and you feel that simply filing a free rebuttal is not sufficient, you can submit the matter to our V.I.P. Arbitration process. The process requires the complaining party to submit a basic complaint form explaining their claim. The complaint is forwarded to the author of the report who is allowed to respond with any proof they have to back up their report. As would be true in court, the complaining party has the burden of proving that a statement is false.

Complaints and responses are then reviewed by one of several neutral and highly experienced arbitrators, one of whom is a retired judge. Other than administering the program, Ripoff Report itself plays no role in deciding the cases submitted for arbitration. If the arbitrator finds that a factual statement in a report is false, that statement will be redacted (removed) from the report, though the report itself will not be removed. Any statements that are not proven to be false will not be removed. In all cases, the title of the report will be updated to reflect that the case has been submitted to arbitration, and a complete copy of the arbitrator's report will be posted above the existing report.

Here are some examples of how reports look after they were submitted to arbitration:

http://www.Ripoffreport.com/insurance-agencies/synergy-capital-insu/synergy-capital-insurance-ma-293d4.htm

http://www.Ripoffreport.com/realtors/savvaidis-associates/savvaidis-associates-property-b8278.htm

Is the program free? Unfortunately, no – there is a cost for participating in the program which covers the arbitrator's fees and our administrative costs, but the program is not expensive compared with other alternatives. While this may not be an ideal solution for everyone, it does give people one more option to consider for disputing reports without the huge cost and delay of litigation.

If you would like to receive more information about the arbitration program, you can send us an email at: Arbitration@RipoffReport.com, or you can review a more detailed explanation of the program here: http://www.Ripoffreport.com/remove-a-report/vip-arbitration-program/ed-magedson-explains-7ad2e.htm

4. The Law You Need To Know – The Communications Decency Act

Because we will not remove reports, Ripoff Report has been sued on many occasions based on the content which our users have created and posted. If you are considering suing Ripoff Report because of a report which you claim is defamatory, you should be aware that to date, Ripoff Report has never lost such a case (with one exception; explained below). This is because of a federal law called the Communications Decency Act or "CDA", 47 U.S.C. § 230. Because this important law is not well known, we want to take a moment to explain the law, and to also explain that the filing of frivolous lawsuits can have serious consequences for those who file them, both parties and their attorneys.

The CDA is part of our federal laws. An excellent Wikipedia article discussing the history of the law can be found here:

http://en.wikipedia.org/wiki/Section_230_of_th e_Communications_Decency_Act

In short, the CDA provides that when a user writes and posts material on an "interactive website" such as Ripoff Report, the site itself cannot, in most cases, be held legally responsible for the posted material. Specifically, 47 U.S.C. § 230(c)(1) states, "No provider or user of an interactive computer service shall be treated as the publisher or speaker of any information provided by another information content provider."

Because the reports on Ripoff Report are authored by users of the site, we cannot be legally regarded as the "publisher or speaker" of the reports contained here, and hence we are not liable for reports even if they contain false or inaccurate information (NOTE: we occasionally create editorial comments and other material, but when we do, this is clearly marked as such). The same law applies to sites like Facebook, MySpace, and CraigsList – users who post information on these sites are responsible for what they write, but the operators of the sites are not.

The reasons for this law are simple. Websites cannot possibly monitor the accuracy of the huge volume of information which their users may choose to post. If an angry plaintiff were permitted to hold a website liable for information that the site did not create, this would stifle free speech as fewer and fewer sites would be willing to permit users to post anything at all. See generally Batzel v. Smith, 333 F.3d 1018, 1027-28 (9th Cir. 2003) (recognizing, "Making interactive computer services and their users liable for the speech of third parties would severely restrict the information available on the Internet. Section 230 [of the CDA] therefore sought to prevent lawsuits from shutting down websites and other services on the Internet.")

Based on the protection extended by the CDA, Ripoff Report has successfully defended more than 20 lawsuits in both state and federal courts. Each time, the courts have consistently found that the CDA shields Ripoff Report from any claims seeking to treat it as the speaker or publisher of information posted by a third party.

Here are just a few recent examples:

•Intellect Art Multimedia, Inc. v. Milewski, 2009 WL 2915273 (N.Y. Sup. Sept. 11, 2009) (claims against Ripoff Report dismissed for failure to state a claim due to CDA immunity)

•GW Equity, LLC v. Xcentric Ventures, LLC, 2009 WL 62173 (N.D. Tex. 2009) (summary judgment entered in favor of Ripoff Report based on CDA immunity)

•Global Royalties, Ltd. v. Xcentric Ventures, LLC, 544 F.Supp.2d 929 (D. Ariz. 2008) (claims against Ripoff Report dismissed pursuant to Fed. R. Civ. P. 12(b)(6) without leave to amend based on CDA immunity)

•Global Royalties, Ltd. v. Xcentric Ventures, LLC, 2007 WL 2949002 (D. Ariz. Oct. 10, 2007) (claims against Ripoff Report dismissed pursuant to Fed. R. Civ. P. 12(b)(6) based on CDA immunity)

•Whitney Info. Network, Inc. v. Xcentric Ventures, LLC, 2008 WL 450095; 2008 U.S. Dist. LEXIS 11632 (M.D. Fla. Feb. 15, 2008) (summary judgment entered in favor of Ripoff Report based on CDA immunity)

So, why should you care about the CDA? Well, it's simple – if someone posts false information about you on Ripoff Report, the CDA prohibits you from holding us liable for the statements which others have written. You can always sue the author if you want, but you can't sue Ripoff Report just because we provide a forum for speech.

Now, to be 100% accurate – some people have said that Ripoff Report DID lose one case in the past, and that's technically almost true. Here's the deal: there was ONE case in 2003 where a predecessor website to Ripoff Report was sued in a foreign country and a default judgment was entered in the plaintiff's favor for more than $27 million "Eastern Caribbean Dollars" (we're not sure how much this would be in U.S. dollars). However, when the plaintiff tried to domesticate that judgment in the United States, we fought it. The case was resolved and the judgment was satisfied without any money being paid. If you think this still counts as a "loss" you're entitled to that opinion but we don't see it that way. NOTE – as explained further below, a new law was enacted in August 2010 which generally prohibits U.S. courts from honoring foreign judgments like this.

5. Other websites say courts have determined Ripoff Report isn't protected by the CDA, who's telling the truth?

In our opinion, the debate between Ripoff Report and our critics isn't even close – we give you the TRUTH and our critics don't. Want an example? Here's a good one…if you find someone who claims that courts have determined we're not protected by the CDA, ask them these two questions:

•What's your authority for that? AND

•Are there any more recent cases which have rejected that authority?

Here's our response to these two questions. When we try to explain what the CDA does and does not cover, some of our less-than-honest critics will cite two cases and claim that in those cases, the court "held" or "found" that Ripoff Report is NOT protected by the CDA. These two cases are MCW, Inc. v. Badbusinessbureau.com, LLC, 2004 U.S. Dist. LEXIS 6678, *(N.D. Tex. 2004), and HyCite Corp. v. Badbusinessbureau.com, 2005 U.S. Dist. LEXIS 38082 (D. Ariz. 2005). If you're looking for a way to successfully sue Ripoff Report, these cases might sound really helpful.

Trust us – they're not. Here's why:

Both cases involved basically the same facts – the plaintiffs alleged that Ripoff Report itself (rather than a third-party user) created false statements about them. Based on these unproven allegations, the courts refused to dismiss the cases under Rule 12(b)(6) of the Federal Rules of Civil Procedure. Does that mean we LOST the case? NO! Does that mean the plaintiff won? NO! Does that mean the courts "held" or "ruled" that we lost CDA immunity? NO!

Because most people reading this page are not lawyers, we need to explain a simple point about civil lawsuits – there's a difference between making an allegation and proving that allegation. You can allege that Donald Trump owes you $1 billion, but unless you have PROOF to support that claim, Mr. Trump isn't going to worry very much.

The decisions in both MCW and HyCite involved allegations, not proof. What does this mean? Well, the courts refused to throw out both cases because the judges determined that if the plaintiffs could prove Ripoff Report actually created the statements at issue, the CDA would not apply. When courts make this type of ruling at the start of a case, it doesn't mean the plaintiff has won or that the plaintiff is likely to win. Rather, this type of technical legal ruling does only one thing – it tests the legal sufficiency of the plaintiff's claims. In so doing, the court cannot review any evidence, and it must assume the allegations are true even if they are not. Based on this hypothetical, the court then determines whether those unproven allegations might support a claim IF the plaintiff can offer evidence to prove their case.

This is why the rulings in both MCW and HyCite are basically meaningless – the decisions were not based on any evidence; they were merely based on unproven allegations. But don't just take our word for it. Look at what other judges have said in more recent decisions.

Bearing in mind that these are old cases (MCW was from 2004 and HyCite was from 2005), in more recent cases judges have reviewed both MCW and HyCite and found both of them to be absolutely irrelevant to our immunity under the CDA. See GW Equity, LLC v. Xcentric Ventures,

LLC, 2009 WL 62173, *4 (N.D. Tex. 2009) (finding MCW did not support the argument that Ripoff Report was not entitled to CDA immunity); Global Royalties, Ltd. v. Xcentric Ventures, LLC, 2007 WL 2949002 (D. Ariz. 2007) (finding plaintiff's reliance on HyCite to be "unavailing").

6. I don't live in the United States; What if I sue Ripoff Report outside the United States?

Sometimes Ripoff Report receives letters from overseas threatening to bring a lawsuit against us in Europe, Canada, the Middle East or other places with laws that don't protect freedom of speech as strongly as the United States does. These letters usually say the same thing: "U.S. law might protect websites such as Ripoff Report, but those laws do not apply in my home country. So, we are going to bring a lawsuit in our country and Ripoff Report won't be able to claim immunity under the CDA." Are these threats effective?

NO. Why? Because Ripoff Report is based in the United States and we have no assets outside the U.S., so any foreign judgment against us would be worthless until the plaintiff brings the judgment here and asks a U.S. court to honor and enforce it. In the past, U.S. judges had some discretion to decide whether to honor or reject foreign judgments, but this is no longer true.

In 2010, the U.S. adopted a new "anti-libel tourism" law, 28 U.S.C. § 4102, which generally prohibits all U.S. courts from honoring foreign libel/defamation judgments if they conflict with the free speech rights guaranteed by our First Amendment. In addition, the new law specifically prohibits U.S. courts from honoring foreign libel/defamation judgments against website operators if the claims at issue would have been barred under U.S. law. See 28 U.S.C. § 4102(c).

7. What if the original author asks us to remove a report? Why doesn't Ripoff Report have to take a report down when the author requests this?

There are many reasons why Ripoff Report does not remove reports even if the original author has asked us to do so. First of all, if someone contacts us and claims to be the author of Report #1234, we have no way of knowing whether they really ARE the author.

Second, as stated above – as a matter of policy, Ripoff Report does not want big companies to bully individuals into asking us to remove their truthful reports. To prevent this, we simply will not agree to remove reports, ever, thus eliminating that incentive.

Third, every time a report is submitted to us, the author must read and agree to the following terms (under "Step 6 – Submit Report"):

"By posting this report/rebuttal, I attest this report is valid. I am giving Ripoff Report irrevocable rights to post it on this website. I acknowledge that once I post my report, it will not be removed, even at my request. Of course, I can always update my report to reflect new developments by clicking on UPDATE." Since this statement is clear, our users should understand that by submitting a report, they are creating a permanent record. If this isn't something they want to do, they should not submit a report in the first place.

8. Specific Answers To Frequently Asked Questions

There's a false report about me on this site!!! What can I do?

As explained above, one thing you can't do is to sue Ripoff Report for material we did not create. Sorry, but the law just does not allow this. You can always sue the person who wrote the report if it contains false and defamatory information about you. Of course, you should talk to an experienced lawyer in your area if you are unsure about your options.

Just because Ripoff Report won't remove reports does not mean you have no options. On the contrary, you can write a rebuttal explaining your position. Rebuttals are 100% free, and we strongly encourage you to use this resource since they can be extremely effective.

If you are a business owner and you discover the report was written by an unhappy customer, do not despair. You can turn that negative into a positive. Use the complaint as an opportunity to make things right with your customer, and ask them to submit an update confirming that their concern has been satisfactorily resolved. Even if the customer won't submit an update, you can write a rebuttal stating what you have done to make things right. As we often say, every business will receive complaints. Customers know that. Having a complaint does not mean your company is bad. It is the manner in which you choose to deal with your customers that will have the biggest impact on your reputation, so treat every complaint as an opportunity to show customers you DO care about treating them well even when things go wrong. Of course, if you don't care about making things right with your customers, that's something the public has a right to know.

If you think a report is fake and/or written by a competitor, feel free to say so in your rebuttal. Your rebuttal can also demand that the customer post some form of proof to back up their story. If the customer fails to do so, that will speak volumes about their credibility (or lack thereof).

If you find that a complaint has been filed against you, the best thing you can do is to post a rebuttal and tell your side of the story. Don't get mad, and don't make threats. Get creative. Explain your side of the story. Explain what your company has done (or is willing to do) to make things right.

If the customer is simply wrong, say so! If you think a report is phony, demand that the customer provide proof that they actually did business with you (by posting a copy of a receipt, etc.) If the customer doesn't respond, this will pretty much be the end of the matter.

Post the names and contact information for favorable references who can testify to the high quality of your business. Provide a summary of any awards your company has won. Offer a link to any outside resources which provide positive information about you and your business.

Ultimately, there are countless ways you can take a negative complaint and turn it into a positive advertisement for your company. As we ALWAYS say: every company, good or bad, will receive complaints. The fact that you have received a complaint is NOT what consumers care about – it's how you handle the complaint that matters.

If I get the original author of a report to send a retraction demand, will Ripoff Report remove the complaint?

We are ALWAYS happy to hear that a dispute has been resolved! If you reach an agreement to resolve a complaint and the original author is willing to retract his/her report, they can easily post the retraction as an update to their report. This is 100% free and it will let the world know that the matter has been handled to the customer's satisfaction. We are always happy to hear about parties resolving their disputes amicably and we strongly encourage authors to post updates any time their complaints have been satisfied.

However, we cannot and will not consider removal requests from anyone, including a request which claims to be from the original author of a report. The reasons for this are explained above, but to summarize them again, we cannot determine which side to a dispute is telling the truth. Although our Terms of Service prohibit users from posting false information, we simply cannot serve as the judge or jury in disputes between two parties. Likewise, if we receive an email from someone claiming to be the author of a report and asking that it be removed, we have no way of knowing if this request is really from the original author, nor do we know if the request is seeking the removal of truthful information solely because of a threat from the person listed in the report.

My lawyer says you have to remove false information upon demand, is that true?

No, for the reasons explained above, that's not true. Under the CDA, Ripoff Report is not liable for the accuracy of statements posted by the users of the site. Therefore, we are not required to remove reports even upon demand.

My lawyer says Ripoff Report has to verify complaints before they are posted and I can sue if you don't, is that true?

In the case of major media sources (i.e., newspapers, etc.), this is generally true; stories must pass through some reasonable level of fact-checking and if they don't, the author and publishers might be liable for any mistakes they make.

Ripoff Report is not *The New York Times* or *The Wall Street Journal* or NBC Nightly News. Those kinds of media have the power, the ability, and therefore the duty to fact-check their stories before they are posted. As to these kinds of mainstream media sources, the law generally does impose some responsibility upon reporters and newspapers to check their stories before publishing them.

This logic works for large, for-profit newspapers, magazines, etc., but it does not translate well for free, user-controlled websites like Ripoff Report which receives thousands of submissions per day, 24 hours a day, 7 days a week, 365 days a year. If Ripoff Report was required to fact-check every report submitted by every user, the site would immediately cease to exist. While some unscrupulous businesses might applaud this, such a reduction in the amount of free speech available online is so un-American that our Congress enacted the CDA to prevent this result.

Someone posted a report which violates Ripoff Report's Terms of Service. Will you remove it?

As explained on this page, although our Terms of Service prohibit users from posting false information, we simply cannot serve as the judge or jury in disputes between two parties. If you contact us and demand that we remove information because you contend that it's false and therefore a violation of our TOS, we have no way to determine if this is true, or if the information is really accurate. These issues have to be determined in court, not by us.

In some cases, if a report contains private information such as a social security number, bank account details/passwords, or threats of violence, we will attempt to redact such material before a report is posted when it is clear that the material is prohibited by our Terms of Service. If such information accidentally gets into a published report, please contact us and we will remove the information if appropriate.

However, if a report contains information which you allege is false, the staff of Ripoff Report cannot simply remove information based on your request because doing so would place us in a position of having to determine which side is telling the truth. Because we cannot make such determinations, if you allege that a report contains false and defamatory statements, you should pursue legal action against the author if you determine such action is warranted.

Someone posted a report which used my trademarks in the title or metatags. Isn't this illegal?

The simple answer is generally NO; using a trademark in a metatag relating to a consumer complaint about the trademark holder is not illegal. However, this area of law is subject to a great deal of confusion, so here are some helpful points you should know.

First, trademark law is a highly specialized area of law which is complicated to say the least. A complete explanation of both federal (Lanham Act) and common-law trademark rules is beyond the scope of this site.

Second, regardless of what particular aspect of trademark law you're dealing with (trademark infringement, trademark dilution, unfair competition, etc.), there is a general requirement that must be present before trademark law will apply – the person who is [mis]using your mark must be a competitor of yours. See Procter & Gamble Company v. Amway Corporation, 242 F.3d 539, 560 (5th Cir. 2001). When someone is NOT your competitor, it is generally not a violation of trademark law for them to say disparaging things about you even if they use your name or other trademarks in the process.

One of the best examples of this is a recent decision called Bosley Medical Institute, Inc. v. Kremer, 403 F.3d 672 (9th Cir. 2005). The basic story of the case goes like this: Bosley Medical offers hair restoration services for balding men. Mr. Kremer was an unhappy former customer who sued Bosley for medical malpractice and lost.

Not content with that outcome, Mr. Kremer started a website called http://www.bosleymedical.com which he filled with statements harshly criticizing Bosley's business. When the company found out about the website, it sued Mr. Kremer for, among other things, trademark infringement because the site was using Bosley Medical's trademarks.

The Ninth Circuit rejected Bosley's claims, holding that because Kremer and Bosley were not competitors, trademark law simply did not apply to the case:

"The dangers that the Lanham Act was designed to address are simply not at issue in this case. The Lanham Act, expressly enacted to be applied in commercial contexts, does not prohibit all unauthorized uses of a trademark. Kremer's use of the Bosley Medical mark simply cannot mislead consumers into buying a competing product – no customer will mistakenly purchase a hair replacement service from Kremer under the belief that the service is being offered by Bosley. Neither is Kremer capitalizing on the goodwill Bosley has created in its mark. Any harm to Bosley arises not from a competitor's sale of a similar product under Bosley's mark, but from Kremer's criticism of their services. Bosley cannot use the Lanham Act either as a shield from Kremer's criticism, or as a sword to shut Kremer up."

Based on the Ninth Circuit's decision in Bosley, unless you operate a business which competes directly with Ripoff Report, and unless

135

a significant number of people viewing Ripoff Report's website would believe that they were actually viewing your website rather than a web forum, then trademark law simply does not apply to prevent the use of trademarks in connection with reports posted on the website.

The same is true of metatags. In case you don't know, metatags are just a series of words (usually keywords) which you cannot see but which are included in the HTML code for most web pages. These tags are used for indexing purposes by search engines such as Google.

When a person creates a Ripoff Report, our software automatically converts the title of the report into metatags based on what the user entered into the title creation form. So, if you created a report about "Acme Corporation" located in "Miami, Florida", these words would be included as metatags so that search engines will accurately index the contents of that page. This isn't a violation of Acme's trademark rights.

It is a common misconception that a trademarked term (i.e., Coca-Cola; McDonald's, Budweiser, etc.) cannot be used in a metatag without the trademark owner's permission. This can be true in some cases, but the mere fact that a trademark is used in a metatag is not per se unlawful; "the mere fact that [a defendant] uses [a plaintiff's] marks in the metatags of its sites and as search-engine keywords does not result in initial interest confusion. [The plaintiff] must show that these uses are deceptive." Designer Skin, L.L.C. v. S & L Vitamins, Inc., 560 F.Supp.2d 811, 818–19 (D. Ariz. 2008).

Again, if a trademark is used in a way that cannot confuse viewers or mislead them into purchasing a product from Company A when they believed they were dealing with Company B, then trademark law generally does not apply to this situation.

Because of this, when a report appears on Ripoff Report and it contains a third-party's trademark in either the title, text of the report, or in metatags, this is not a violation of trademark law because no consumer viewing the site will be confused about the fact that they are not looking at the trademark owner's webpage. Absent such competitive harm, trademark law is not concerned with preventing the use of trademarks for purposes such as criticism, discussion, and other acts of free speech.

If I file a lawsuit against Ripoff Report, will that get my complaint removed?

No. Ripoff Report is not liable for statements posted by a third party, and it has never lost a case involving such statements, so it will not remove complaints even if you sue.

Filing a lawsuit will, however, guarantee the removal of one thing – a LOT of money from your wallet and into an attorney's pocket.

I heard that Ripoff Report pays Google to get higher rankings in search results, is that true?

No. This is 100% false.

Considering that Google is one of the largest, most successful, and most well-respected Internet companies on the planet, this rumor is hard for even the most cynical/skeptical to believe. Why would a multi-billion-dollar company like Google give preferential treatment to a relatively small, controversial site like Ripoff Report? IT WOULDN'T, PEOPLE!

The reasons that some websites show up higher on Google than others is a complete mystery, at least to Ripoff Report. In fact, although Google is happy to give a general explanation of how its ranking system works, the actual algorithms used by Google to determine page ranking are some of the most closely guarded trade secrets out there.

NOTE – some people have claimed that posting a rebuttal on our site somehow causes reports to appear higher in Google than they otherwise would. For that reason, these skeptics have suggested that filing a rebuttal is a BAD idea. We have two responses to this.

First, we have never seen any proof that this claim is true and there is a lot of anecdotal evidence to show this claim is false. Consider this – in most cases even if a report does NOT contain any rebuttals, it will still show up very high in Google's search results. Will posting a rebuttal make any difference to that ranking? Maybe yes and maybe no, but this leads to our second point...

Second, if posting a rebuttal makes a report more visible in Google, why not use that to your advantage? How? By using the rebuttal as a form of free advertising for your company!

Look, Google earns billions of dollars a year in advertising revenue from companies who are desperate to show up on Page 1. If posting a FREE rebuttal gets your company's name on the first page of Google, why not use this as an opportunity to shine?! For example, regardless of how accurate a report might be, why not post a free rebuttal that says something like this: "Hi, I'm the President of the company listed in this report, and I want to show you how dedicated I am to 100% customer satisfaction. To prove this, we are currently offering a 20% discount to anyone who prints this report and brings it in to our store (or mentions Ripoff Report when placing an order). Thank you for giving us a chance to show you what an excellent company we are!"

Other websites have said that Ed Magedson writes reports and titles to reports, is that true?

ABSOLUTELY NOT! Many people have worked very hard to spread this false story, but in the end, it's just not true.

Here's the truth:

When an author writes a report, they also create a title for their report at the same time. The title, category, and report contents are ALL chosen and created by the person who drafted a report, not by us. If you have any trouble believing this, just create a free account then log in and file a report. You will see exactly how it works, and you'll see that what you write is what is posted, nothing more and nothing less.

Now, to be clear: Ripoff Report DOES make changes to reports only in limited circumstances when necessary to remove material that violates our guidelines (i.e., child pornography, clear threats of violence, etc.) Whenever this is done, the change is clearly noted in the report itself.

Similarly, the Editor of Ripoff Report will sometimes add comments/updates to reports, usually when a company has specifically asked for this by joining Ripoff Report Corporate Advocacy Program. Again, when this is done, the comments are CLEARLY noted as coming from the Editor of the site so there's no confusion about the source.

Finally, in some very rare instances we have posted our own reports when we have something extremely important to say. Here's one such example: http://www.Ripoffreport.com/attorneys-legal-services/kenton-j-hutcherson/kenton-j-hutcherson-hutcherso-6afd8.htm. As you can see, it is clearly indicated that this report was posted by Ripoff Report.

I want the name of someone who posted an anonymous report about me. How can I get that?

This is a somewhat technical issue, so we created a separate page for it here: http://www.Ripoffreport.com/ConsumersSayThankYou/FalseReport.aspx

I Heard That Ripoff Report Is An Extortion Scheme; What's Up With That?

You may have read on other websites that Ripoff Report authors reports or headings to reports, or that we write fake reports and then ask for money in order to remove them (hence, the claim that the site is committing "extortion").

These kinds of allegations are false statements made by companies who have been the subject of numerous complaints on Ripoff Report. Some of these companies have been the subject of government investigations and have had to pay hundreds of thousands in restitution and fines. Some have since been arrested and some have been closed down.

Because some of these unethical companies have found that they cannot use legal means to remove reports, some have tried resorting to illegal means to get reports taken down. These methods have included making death threats against us, harassing our staff, attacking our website with spam, DDOS attacks, making false claims in lawsuits, and creating websites which claim to reveal the "true story" about Ripoff Report. These misguided individuals often use one or more of the following false allegations:

• Ripoff Report, or its founder Ed Magedson, are "under investigation by the FBI" or another federal agency;

• Ripoff Report is run by criminals;

• There is a "class-action" lawsuit pending against Ripoff Report;

• Ripoff Report is an "extortion scheme" because the site writes fake reports and then demands money to remove them;

As you may have guessed, these statements are all 100% false – but don't take our word for it. If you see a website making these kinds of claims, try to find contact information for the person who created the site and ask them what proof they have to support their claims. If you don't get a response, that might be a hint.

Is the Corporate Advocacy Program an Extortion Scheme?

Since the best lies are those which contain a little bit of truth, you should understand that Ripoff Report does offer a service called the "Corporate Advocacy Program" (or "CAP"), and many of the extortion claims out there are based on false explanations of what the CAP program is all about. In order to avoid confusion, here's the truth about this program:

If a company has received one or more Ripoff Reports, that business always has the option of posting free rebuttals and/or working with its customers to try to make things right. Hopefully, when a customer's complaint is resolved, that person will do the right thing and submit their own follow-up to explain that the company stepped up and corrected the problem. When a company has just one or two complaints, many choose to handle this process themselves with their own staff and at their own expense.

However, when a company receives lots and lots of complaints, the time spent dealing with each one can become overwhelming. That's where our CAP program comes in.

When a company asks for our assistance, through our Corporate Advocacy Program we agree to work with the business to reach out to their customers to help resolve any disputes. Whether a company has 10 complaints or 500 complaints, we assist our CAP members by contacting each and every unhappy customer to try to resolve the dispute in an amicable manner. We only offer this service to companies who are willing to agree that they must make things right with their customers – PERIOD. Ripoff Report UPDATES (but never removes) those reports, reflecting the member business' commitment to customer satisfaction. This becomes a win-win for both company and customer alike.

Of course, like anything else worth having, our CAP program is not free. Someone needs to pay to keep the lights on and the servers running, and so we charge a reasonable fee for our time and expenses. If a company can show that it lacks the resources to afford our standard rates, we are glad to offer our services for a reduced price based on the company's financial condition.

So is the CAP program really "extortion"? NO, but don't take our word for it. Instead, please read the 53-page ruling issued by a federal court in Los Angeles on July 19, 2010 in which the court found that the Corporate Advocacy Program was NOT extortion because: "The offer to help Plaintiffs restore their reputation and facilitate resolution with the complainants in exchange for a fee does not constitute a threat under California Penal Code § 519." You can read the court's entire ruling   here: http://www.scribd.com/doc/34667624/Asia-Economic-Institute-LLC-v-Xcentric-Ventures-LLC-Order-Granting-Partial-Summary-Judgment

I Know the CDA Protects Ripoff Report, But I Am Going to Sue Anyway!

If you have read all of the above information and still want to file a lawsuit against us, there are some other points you need to know.

First, Rule 11 of the Federal Rules of Civil Procedure, and each state court's rules, generally require that all pleadings, including initial Complaints, must be presented in good faith, after a reasonable investigation into the facts and the law, and not made for an improper purpose such as harassment. What this means in plain English is that if you file a lawsuit which you know contains false claims, or if you sue without first conducting a reasonable investigation as to the law as it may pertain to the facts of your case

145

(such as determining the identity of the author of the report(s) you are concerned about), you and/or your attorney can be subject to serious sanctions at the judge's discretion. Many who have sued settled with us and some have paid some or all of our attorney's fees. Other times we have defended the cases for years running up large legal bills for both sides. Either way, we never paid out a dime in settlement or damages to anyone who has sued us.

In addition to penalties a judge may issue, those who would threaten us need to be aware of another law which imposes civil liability on anyone who files a frivolous lawsuit. This claim is known as "wrongful use of civil proceedings" and it is defined by § 674 of the Restatement (Second) of Torts as follows:

(a) he acts without probable cause, and primarily for a purpose other than that of securing the proper adjudication of the claim in which the proceedings are based, and

(b) except when they are ex parte, the proceedings have terminated in favor of the person against whom they are brought.

Because Ripoff Report is immune from liability under the CDA for defamation-based and related claims, any suit that seeks to impose liability for the speech of our users is, by definition, an action brought "without probable cause". We encourage the prompt and fair resolution of disputes between Ripoff Report authors and those who are the subject of Ripoff Reports. However, Ripoff Report wants to be clear that it accepts no liability for the speech of its users, and it will vigorously defend any litigation brought against us which seeks to circumvent the CDA. In addition, any suit filed against us without probable cause may subject the complaining party and/or their attorneys to liability in the State of Arizona for wrongful use of civil proceedings. We don't mean to sound harsh, but if you knowingly file a frivolous lawsuit against us, regardless of where your case is filed, you and/or your lawyers can be subject to a lawsuit in Arizona in which a jury could, if appropriate, award both substantial compensatory and punitive damages against you.

Finally, you need to be aware that if you file a lawsuit simply to harass us, not only will this not work, it will very likely end up being EXTREMELY expensive for you. Due to the number of meritless cases we have had to defend, Ripoff Report has adopted a very strict policy about lawsuits – once Ripoff Report is forced to appear in a case, it will not stipulate to a dismissal of the case unless the party who filed the action agrees to pay Ripoff Report's attorney fees. There will be no exceptions. If you conduct a thorough investigation BEFORE you sue and you believe you have a valid case despite the CDA, it is your right to pursue your case and prove it in court. However, once you file a lawsuit, be prepared to either take it all the way to a decision on the merits or pay Ripoff Report's attorney fees because Ripoff Report will not stipulate to a dismissal without compensation.

Back to me

Feeling a little intimidated? Can you tell the difference between fact and fiction? Every great lie has to have a scattering of truth.

Chapter 23. Ripoff Report exposed, or is it?

Fact or fiction, man or myth? Well, like all good stories Ed Magedson of Ripoff Report's story is no different, the lines between fact and fiction are blurred. Almost impossible to tell what's real and what's not. I dare say after talking to Ed Magedson and studying his business model that he's more brilliant than most will ever admit. I had ended up in the unfortunate place of being introduced to Ripoff Report a few years ago out of the blue. Three, two, one, boom!

What just hit us? It was Ripoff Report straight out of nowhere to Page 1 of Google, third spot down was "Ripoff Report – Fraud, Scam, Complaints." We had been in business for roughly 15 years without blemish and then some young guy – a disgruntled kid really, who didn't last a complete day in the office decided to post an angry and fictitious rendition of our company on Ripoff Report.

Baptism by fire! Within a couple of days if I remember correctly three or four postings by anonymous parties had emerged and all scandalous in nature. Here starts the game and it's a brilliant game potentially devised and run by Ed Magedson.

You do your research into Ripoff Report and you find there are some wild statements made about Ed Magedson, such as "felon, wanted by FBI, extortionist, crazy, weirdo guy in hiding somewhere abroad, hiding out, never lost a lawsuit." The list goes on, page after page of none-too-pleasant references on Ed Magedson and Ripoff Report.

When first attacked, you search the Ripoff Report site located at www.Ripoffreport.com and you try to distinguish if there has been a mistake. Is Ed Magedson a consumer advocate? Has there been some error made and can it be undone?

Our first response was to do nothing out of fear. Maybe it will go away on its own. Fear of doing something to make it worse! Eventually and after much contemplation (about a years' worth) we realized that paralyzation was not the answer. We were losing business and rapidly. We went from feeling in control to out of control in a few short weeks. It was time to do something!

I wanted to call Ripoff Report but found no phone number listed. Instead the contact us page on Ripoff Report opened up an email box with the recipient as Editor@Ripoffreport.com. So I sent an email. Ed Magedson and I talked numerous times over the next few months about how to fix the problem we had of being discussed on Ripoff Report. We talked straight talk and small talk.

Mostly I listened and Ed talked. I knew he could do whatever he wanted to us. The Internet had given him that power, or so I thought.

Remaining calm was my goal in each communication over the phone and email. I succeeded although the same wasn't always true of Ed. I wanted to disarm Ed in the hope that at some time he would loosen his grip on us.

Talking to Ed was like playing a game of chess against someone who's absolutely better at it than you. Ed Magedson beats you 10 out of 10 times. He also decided the stakes. We had no say in the stakes and Ed got us to bet the house every time. But knowing that I had to learn how he plays in order to stand a chance against him, I had to play again and again. I can honestly say I have been through some stuff in my life which could have or should have left me battle-weak or weary. This was the first time I felt helpless – a victim. I ended up trying to get to know my attacker in the hope that I would become more human to him.

Ed Magedson outsmarted us all and until a court says differently he did it legally. That doesn't mean I agree with his ethics or his business model. But in the most capitalistic country of them all this is pure capitalism at work. And I don't necessarily like that either. You see, the Internet didn't give Ed Magedson the power as suggested by *The Phoenix New Times* writer Sarah Fenske in her article "The Real Ripoff

Report" – the door was opened by the Telecommunications Act of 1996, Title V, Sec 230. Ed Magedson was smart enough to take advantage of the opportunity given to him by the U.S. Senate.

Ed Magedson can talk passionately about being a consumer advocate and he's believable – mostly. There are without doubt companies listed on Ripoff Report that deserve to be there and for possible consumers of the products and services of those less-than-reputable companies Ripoff Report does a great service. This is where Ed starts to outsmart us. He knows the best fiction has a grain of truth thrown in.

Here's where we all got it wrong: Ed Magedson knows if we stay angry enough at him, we will endeavor to beat him in the press, online and in court.

You can't beat him directly in the social arena. Faced with making a decision to purchase a company's products or services, who would ignore a line that states "Fraud, Ripoff, Scam, Complaints"? Who would want to take the pressure of an "I told you so", and what might it cost us? We just don't run those kinds of risks unless we are given overwhelming evidence to suggest a different outcome than the one Ripoff suggests, and that in itself changes and influences the perception of risk.

So Ed can always point to the good work he does and offer an apology if your company got listed by someone. After all, he didn't write the post, did he?

Here we go again; more of the same. Blurred lines between fact and fiction. It has been suggested that others with less than the best of intentions have written posts on behalf of Ripoff Report. During a legal discovery, one individual suspected of being a complaint poster was also suspected of having over one hundred aliases to which he was suspected of posting from. As for any actual tie to Ed Magedson or Ripoff Report I can't say. I can say that of the three or four postings about the company I was with at the time, to the best of our abilities to determine the identity of the posters (we joined the Corporate Advocacy Program) only one was ever established.

Why doesn't Ed or Ripoff Report remove postings? Think of the allegations that would come up and secondly if they do remove postings they open themselves up to technical problems that they are currently protected against under Sec 230.

Thinking of suing Ripoff Report; why not? Has Ripoff Report, Ed Magedson or Xcentric (corporate name) ever lost a lawsuit? Depends on how you define lost! Ed Magedson has a talented group of attorneys that do this stuff all day. They defend Ed et al all day and they're good at it. They have more practice, I would imagine, than most defending online defamation amongst other related suits. The chances are that his attorneys are far better prepared than yours. To make a play on words, Ed doesn't lose lawsuits; he makes and takes calculated risks and settles when he has to.

Think about it from a return on investment. Some notoriety is good for Ripoff Report. I'd hate to sound like an advocate for Ed but I am on this one. From firsthand knowledge the law is on his side until you can prove he operated outside of the law. If you want to blow tens of thousands of dollars on a worthless endeavor, go ahead. We were suing a smaller copycat site. While building a case against Ripoff Report we thought we would educate and prepare with the smaller fish, before proving our arguments on the granddaddy of them all, Ripoff, Ed and Xcentric. The smaller fish turned out to be deadly.

Plain and simple, the Telecommunications Act of 1996, Title V commonly called the Communications Decency Act, Sec 230, does a really good job of protecting the defendant. Beyond your wildest dreams, it does a good job!

We had a top-tier legal firm representing us. It didn't make the difference we thought it would! When the law isn't in your favor, all the smarts in the world aren't going to change the outcome. It would have cost less and we would have realized we were on a road to nowhere sooner if we had used not just a top law firm, but more importantly a firm that understood and focused on online law and defamation.

I should have known I had a problem when it was the legal intrigue and shock, not the established legal expertise on the subject matter that was the conversation had by the attorneys with me. The fact that the law firm was considered a top firm made the ownership of the company feel more secure. Everything was breaking new ground. We were to find a new way to win. We didn't. We ran out of steam. It was going to be a two-year battle at best.

We were being targeted now by the spin machine of the opposing attorneys, who made it publicly seem like we were a corporate giant going after the little guy and squashing the freedom of speech. We were about one hundred employees and that doesn't make for much of a giant. Let someone paint the freedom-crushing target on *your* back and see what kind of feedback *you* get!

One word of caution, or rather a few: remember if you ask an attorney whether you stand a chance in court or have a leg to stand on, you are technically asking commissioned salespeople. I do not mean that in any derogatory way. There are bad, good and great attorneys who can help; some are just good salespeople who will find a way to say without guarantees that they believe they can have a favorable outcome.

Attorneys are responsible for bringing in revenue too. I really do know some of the best attorneys that couldn't be any more honest with a client about the stakes, and I've met plenty of pure salesmen with a law degree. Find a great attorney!

Based on my research into various cases filed against Ed Magedson et al, he has about a two-year path through the court system before he settles if he has to. That's two years of potentially major legal fees (try $200,000) and a drain on everyone involved. If I look at it from Ripoff's perspective, I have to weigh up the cost benefit analysis of a very small company taking me to court. If I have no way of recovering my costs to defend the suit, it would be strategically and financially advantageous to settle early under a nondisclosure.

My personal theory after talking to Ed is that you will never get him on a plane and into a courtroom. So if you can force Ed to attend an out-of-Arizona court hearing sooner than later, you may reach an early settlement. It's just a theory! I'd really love to know.

Getting back on track: we determined that filing a rebuttal on Ripoff was a dangerous thing because we didn't know who we were talking to, and it was obvious the attack on us was malicious. Remember, we had operated for years without a blemish. We looked into the Corporate Advocacy Program (CAP). Is it extortion? I guess that depends on where you sit.

If I were Ed Magedson and I truly believe what I am doing is acting as a consumer advocate, it doesn't matter whether I am a consumer advocate or not. It's more of the fuzzy line stuff. Is he a consumer advocate or not? It again depends on the perspective. If I am an advocate, I understand that a couple of things can happen:

1. Innocent companies may get caught up in the disturbance
2. Companies should have an opportunity to redeem themselves if the problems were not criminal, and they can learn from their mistakes

This is basically what Ed Magedson said to me, "I will become the marketing arm for the company that has the negative posting and I'll charge you for the service as would any other service company." Are you basking in his glory? Brilliant!

Ok, "say you're sorry for your sins and that you are now doing everything you can to make sure you don't do it again." What if you didn't commit any sins? "Say you're sorry for your sins and that you are now doing everything you can to make sure you don't do it again." It was like admitting to your guilt when you are innocent in order to get less time!

Does the word 'victimized' come to mind?

We ended up writing a check for a few thousand dollars to the Corporate Advocacy Program and I went on to shape the content of the "Investigation Report" under the guidance of Ed Magedson. Ed was very convinced of his theory that the tag or headline still had to be sensational or people wouldn't read it. And after all "if it came from Ripoff, if Ripoff Report were saying we were to be trusted or words similar in fashion, then how could it be bad for us"?

There never was an investigation of any kind. I wrote every word of the report with Ed Magedson via email communications. I still have every email message Ed and I sent to each other.

So *is it* extortion? Ed provides a service by which companies are to implement customer service strategies that would better the customer experience. I don't know what those strategies are other than setting up an email box for people to communicate directly from Ripoff Report to your email box. Another strategy of the Corporate Advocacy Program was that before any new posting would go public on Ripoff Report, Ed or

158

staff would let the poster know their identity would be shared with us in order to clear up any problems.

We in turn would have an opportunity to address any problem. What do you suppose happened from there? No more activity. Zero! The activity which was supposedly coming from outside of Ripoff stopped. So was it because the activity wasn't independent of Ripoff, or was it because the anonymity was removed?

Ed is able to say that being a part of the Corporate Advocacy Program reduces the number of complaints and that's good for everyone.

That was, I'm assuming, Ed's perspective and now here's mine:

Ed Magedson might just be a complete narcissist,and I'll bet he's ok with the opinion!

Chapter 24. Narcissist, according to Wikipedia and the DSM:

Some people diagnosed with a narcissistic personality disorder are characterized by exaggerated feelings of self-importance. They have a sense of entitlement and demonstrate grandiosity in their beliefs and behavior. They have a strong need for admiration, but lack feelings of empathy.

Symptoms of this disorder, as defined by the DSM-IV-TR, include:

- Expects to be recognized as superior and special, without superior accomplishments

- Expects constant attention, admiration and positive reinforcement from others

- Envies others and believes others envy him/her

- Is preoccupied with thoughts and fantasies of great success, enormous attractiveness, power, intelligence

- Lacks the ability to empathize with the feelings or desires of others

- Is arrogant in attitude and behavior

• Has expectations of special treatment that are unrealistic

Other symptoms in addition to the ones defined by DSM-IV-TR include: Is interpersonally exploitative, i.e., takes advantage of others to achieve his or her own ends.

Like so many businesses, we never did anything wrong in order to end up on Ripoff Report in the first place. It is impossible to correct something that wasn't incorrect. Can we improve customer interactions? Absolutely! I'd be a fool to think the customer experience or customer service can't be improved. It will never be good enough to overcome every obstacle human beings on both sides of the relationship can throw at you. But do we strive to make every experience a good one? Should you make every reasonable effort to systematically control – and therefore predict – the outcome of those interactions? Yes!

We were put in a position as we saw it, and felt it, of being blackmailed, victimized, and even in some ways violated.

Corporate Advocacy Program or death? As Eddie Izzard says, "I'll take death please." Of course you take the Corporate Advocacy Program! You have little chance of winning a lawsuit – it may take two years or more – it's very expensive, currently you are being accused of being a scam, fraud, with complaints and a headline on Google's Page 1 of the most sensational and damaging description, revenues are dropping as a result, new employees are questioning who they are working for, recruiting is now a problem. Oh, I don't know: "Death please!"

Or, under duress you can pay an agreed amount of money, agree to do a better job, help write an investigation report that says Ripoff Report completed an investigation, change the headline to be slightly more positive than it was and most importantly get a heads up if anyone is going to write a post again, which they never did!

What would you call it? We had a two-year agreement under the Corporate Advocacy Program and while it stopped any further attacks, it didn't make a difference to the damage that still existed because of Ripoff Report.

Copycats and crazy people. General opinion is if you're on Ripoff Report it doesn't matter what it says, you are guilty of something to someone. There is simply no smoke without fire. We would have clients and prospects tell us they cannot associate or be associated with us because of Ripoff Report's reputation and our relationship with them. No one cared who was telling the truth; any relationship to Ripoff was seen as a negative.

We suffered all kinds of copycat sites grabbing information from Ripoff Report. Before long a number of sites trying to copy Ripoff's format had expanded on their anonymous views of us. Strangely enough one such site was Complaintsboard.com. This site was rumored to be Ripoff Report's sister company held under Xcentric. It makes perfect sense if I'm Ed. Duplicate the effort and go for market share.

As the agreement for the Corporate Advocacy Program was with Xcentric and not Ripoff Report directly, when the same content on Ripoff Report ended up on Complaintsboard I flagged their legalize, made copies of the disclosure including the name within their site content of "Xcentric" and sent it to Ed asking if there had been a mistake made as the terms of our agreement were not being honored.

While Ed claimed to not know anything about Complaintsboard, the content was immediately removed. Again, fuzzy lines between fact and fiction.

Ripoff Report's anonymous postings falsely accused most members of the management and ownership of having criminal records and being allegedly under investigation for fraud. The company itself (not a person) was even falsely accused of raping some young girl; the list goes on. To my amazement enough people believed the false stories so convincingly they could not, and would not, accept any other version. It only takes a drop of color to change a bathtub full of water! The absolute truth is that we were never involved in anything unethical or immoral.

I may be a slow learner but it took me about four years of studying the problems surrounding the issues of Ed Magedson and Ripoff Report to come out with some clear understanding of the real problems and solutions.

In my opinion Ed Magedson is a showman. He may prefer to be seen as a quirky, eccentric (Xcentric), easy to hate, paranoid guy. He may have deliberately lit fires under his own bad press in order to create press. He is certainly talented enough to create a bad boy persona. No one knows better than Ed what sells.

If Ed's persona of evangelist for consumer advocacy fails, everything else comes crashing down around him. I think he believes that as long as he is true to that ideal everything else is fair game. "This is business, I play within the rules and the rules say I can do what I do."

He has been one step ahead of us all. He has managed to keep the attention on him which has kept the focus off Ripoff Report. Why? Because without public or online attention Ripoff Report doesn't exist.

I believe it's really about advertising dollars. Heck, let's purify that comment, shall we? I believe it's *all* about dollars! How valuable is the Ripoff Report site? It generates a high volume of page visits every day and that's worth a premium to advertisers.

Ed Magedson, Ripoff Report and Xcentric, just like the copycat sites, make the vast majority of their income from advertising placed on their sites. Ed makes hundreds of thousands, possibly millions, from the Corporate Advocacy Program. Everything else is just the lure to keep you coming. The sensationalism, the spin, the noise; it is all designed to keep his site, Ripoff Report, firmly up there where the advertisers are willing to pay a premium for an opportunity to get in front of its audience. And that's brilliant!

Ed Magedson is a great chess player. He even managed to keep most of us playing on the wrong boards. We figured Google must be to blame when we couldn't figure out how to beat Ed on his own board. We tried learning from some new kids called Reputation Management but they make up the rules as they go and then blame Google when it doesn't work. Some SEO folks still want us to move to a pretty board that wasn't made to handle this game. Most PR, social media and marketing companies haven't figured out yet that they should be playing this game and how.

And too many attorneys are playing the game without reading the rules first.

The business owner will one day figure out that all along they held the board and most of its pieces. Now they just have to figure out how to use them.

Chapter 25. Yelp!

As Reported in *The Boston Channel*: "30 Percent of Online Reviews Could Be Fake."

BOSTON – Millions of people use online review sites to find a good area restaurant or other services. One of the oldest and biggest is Yelp. They say their site helps consumers and businesses. But some business owners say it's losing them customers.

Heather Perrone owns Jae 3 Salon in Medfield. She welcomes feedback but says certain reviews on Yelp are unfair, untrue and bad for business.

"As a small business owner, I think anything negative hurts you," said Perrone. "I had this employee work for me for a long time. She voluntarily left and her friend felt the need to post a review on the Yelp site which was not factual and had personal and private information in it," she said.

Yelp is one of many review sites consumers can go to about a restaurant or salon or store. 63 million people logged on to Yelp in one month, according to the company. Yelp said the service is great for customers and businesses.

But businesses don't sign up for the listings. They just appear from a database. In an email, one business owner wrote to Newscenter 5 to say, "I am losing business and customers because Yelp mistakenly posted my business as closed."

Yelp said that only happens when a business owner doesn't update their address. As for reviews, they say their review filter protects businesses from "fake, shill, or malicious reviews."

An animated video on their website explains the filter process. "It takes reviews from the most trustworthy and most established sources, and takes the less trustworthy sources out," the narrator says.

The algorithmic system is designed to weed out phony reviews that a business might ask for or pay people to write. But Perrone said they also filter out positive, authentic reviews. Those are relegated to the bottom of the page where a user has to open them. And they are listed as not a part of Yelp's rating system.

"In my experience I'm not seeing where the checks and balances are," said Perrone. "I'm not sure we are really validating the information that gets across," she said.

Other review sites like Citysearch and Trip Advisor either have or are exploring review filters. But some businesses say the sites should do more to protect them from misinformation, especially since they never asked for the publicity.

Yelp told Newscenter 5 their automated review filter system and strict set of review guidelines and terms of service ensures people can trust the content. Otherwise, they said, Yelp would be of no benefit to consumers or businesses.

Chapter 26. Better Business Bureau (BBB)

When you've been around since 1912 you must be doing something right, and they are, but it's not without some well-deserved criticism.

The Good

The Better Business Bureau (BBB) has been a trusted source for information since 1912. Prior to the Internet, if you wanted to check out a company your best bet was your local chapter of the BBB. I can accept that their business model (and it is a for profit business) was focused on providing honest and objective feedback to the public about the businesses within their communities.

It's a business and businesses have natural flaws. Its membership pays for the right to be a member. The organization of the BBB wants to increase its membership which would be in conflict with giving a company a bad rating – hence the giant flaw!

The model still doesn't give me reason to throw out the whole BBB because of its flaw. I truly believe that for the most part the BBB serves the communities well – but not perfectly.

I'm not sure where you live, but where I live the police do for the most part a great job. I don't expect perfection – it's tough making perfect decisions all the time. The police force in Chicago has roughly 13,500 officers. Ninety-nine percent (99%) of them never make it into the media for doing good things or for doing their job (and they do a great job, most of the time). The remaining one percent (1%) really does a number on our perception of the other ninety-nine percent (99%) though. Would I throw out the ninety-nine percent (99%) because of the one percent (1%)? Heck no!

The same is true of the companies that claim membership with the BBB. Historically the BBB has brought a level of trust and integrity to businesses that would be hard to establish without them. There are a vast number of businesses that fight hard to legitimately earn and keep positive membership with the BBB. It's good for their business and it's good for their reputation. One percent (1%) will always find a way to take advantage of any system.

The Bad

So what happens when a company has a bad reputation with the BBB? I can't speak for every chapter of the BBB but there is discussion enough to question whether some chapters are losing sight of their main focus of public awareness, by skipping over the bad reports to leave its member companies with a more positive rating than it maybe deserves.

The BBB changed its rating system a few years ago from one which rated companies as "Satisfactory" or "Unsatisfactory" to one which gives out letter grades.

Skipping over or minimizing problems reported to the BBB about the smallest percent of member companies in order to keep other members happy threatens the trust the public puts in the BBB.

The Ugly

Since moving to the letter grade, members and non-members have allegedly been given substantially lower letter grades for nonpayment of fees or services to the BBB.

If a rating system is to work it cannot artificially be used to sway perception toward a group for the benefit of the rating body.

Future

I think the BBB is going through some challenges right now as they, and we, try to figure out how to make the right choices given this new media and new competition for our products and services.

The BBB is still a great place to help build a reputation. It's still a great place to review a company – just don't stop at the letter grade.

Chapter 27: Reputation monitoring – don't be an idiot!

Monitor – To observe, watch, check on over a period of time.

There are a number of tools aimed at reputation monitoring – from free tools to tools that run into the hundreds of dollars each month.

Why monitor?

Well plain and simple, if there is a conversation that's going on about you, or something that's important to you, it's best you know about it sooner than later. There will be nothing negative in the majority of online mentions for the terms or names you monitor, and that's great.

It's not just the negative you need to know about as soon as possible. You need to know about all mentions: the tone, where it's heading, on what kind of site the term shows up, the purpose of the site.

Google Alerts (www.google.com/alerts) is the simplest and cheapest of Google Search early warning systems. It's relatively easy to set up, free to use and it sends new mentions for the searches you save into a profile to your email as often as you like. It doesn't really offer any filters and it is

174

the basics of a monitoring system. It is still suitable for most individuals and small businesses.

I've used Google Alerts for years and it hasn't missed a beat.

Be careful when looking for reputation-monitoring tools and don't pay for a system you don't need. There are plenty of reputation management companies selling something you can get for free!

There are monitoring systems that can monitor every social media account and search engine for you. If you're a celebrity, terrific, I get that you need to monitor every channel. If you're not a celebrity, a more complex monitoring system is really just an excuse to dip into your pocket.

Reputation-monitoring tools are early warning systems like radar is to aircraft. Radar only sees what's already there. It doesn't see what's going to happen or where. Understand that online reputation monitoring does not, and cannot, prevent online criticism.

Used correctly, a good reputation-monitoring system in good hands allows the user to implement defensive strategies that influence the outcome of the reputation being managed. And that helps me sleep at night.

Chapter 28. Conclusion

Reputation management isn't something you just contract someone else to handle for you. Reputation management begins internally. It means doing things the right way. All businesses should be keeping to higher standards and delivering increased customer satisfaction. Every business has enough to do to keep their reputation intact when they're doing a great job of servicing their customers and employees.

Customer dissatisfaction, and employee dissatisfaction, have now found a safe and powerful place to scream their real, justified opinions to the world. But there's no gatekeeper on who's real or what's real.

Add a third component of business competition to the quandary. Not all businesses play by ethical standards. There are plenty of people who will work to gain a competitive advantage over your business, any way they can. They may not be prepared to put in the time and effort to build their own reputation, and instead take the lazy way of making themselves look better by making you look worse. One of the ways they can do that is to destroy your reputation online. Reviews can be bought, sold and falsified.

The forth component is the troll. The troll is someone looking for a target. It's the equivalent to a stalker, a crank caller. The troll has no agenda other than to create mayhem for you. When they choose you and you don't have your customers and employees to defend you, you'll learn what it's like to feel violated.

Reputation management isn't something you outsource. It should be part of your everyday, how you do business.

The information in this book paints an accurate picture of the challenges, sales pitches and philosophies around online reputation management. I hope you'll think long and hard about how your customers and employees see you and your business. I hope you'll find a way to tap into the goodwill you've created and worked so hard to build. Move that goodwill to an online forum before your reputation is challenged.

If you already have a reputation challenge, I hope this has helped to provide answers to the many questions you have. I hope you're able to learn from my years of experience about the sales pitches you're going to face.

The realities of dealing with the challenge, philosophies and attitudes of the challengers. Nothing about reputation management is simple. It's easier to be a target when you don't recognize what makes you an easy target. It's harder to defend your reputation when you don't know what others are trying to gain or take from you.

If you are reading this before your reputation is challenged, you've now been given a body of knowledge and experience that will allow you to make more informed decisions about how to protect your reputation, and influence those who have influence over your reputation.

Change never happens fast enough for those that are oppressed in some way by laws that defend the oppressor. Was the Telecommunications Act of 1996, Title V, commonly called the Communications Decency Act, Sec 230, meant to create a safe harbor for abusers of free speech? I don't think so!

But what about the protections of all freemen? You know the whole Constitution, Bill of Rights, liberty and justice for all freemen thing. The American Declaration of Independence that so many herald as being drawn from England's Magna Carta – written in 1215 – which lays out the first real outline of civil liberties; it was soon misinterpreted from its intended use. The Magna Carta was only intended to represent an agreement between the barons or noblemen and the King of England. The rest of us were still screwed!

The word "free man" wasn't used to describe most of us. Freemen were only the noblest and richest of men. The rest of us mere peasants, also called villains, were ignored. The

Magna Carta didn't apply to us. We weren't freemen!

What's my point? The Magna Carta, America's Bill of Rights and other important pieces of legislation don't happen overnight. These documents are still subject to debate and interpretation today. They will continue to be for as long as we exist. The Internet is still in its infancy and so are the laws that govern its use. It takes time and struggle to find a balance in law. When that balance comes, I fully expect that freedom of speech will remain intact.

Good luck managing your reputation!